PURE SEX

Tony Payne & Phillip D. Jensen

Pure Sex

St Matthias Press Ltd ACN 067 558 365
PO Box 225, Kingsford, NSW 2032
AUSTRALIA

Ph (02) 9663 1478; Fax (02) 9662 4289
International Ph +61-2-9663 1478; Fax +61-2-9662 4289
E-mail: matmedia@ozemail.com.au

ISBN 1 876326 07 7

Cover design & typesetting by Joy Lankshear Design Pty Ltd.

Contents

Introduction

AN INTRODUCTION to a book on sex is rather like the wrapping paper around a child's Christmas present. It will be very quickly disposed of in order to get to the excitements that lie inside. Before the reader rushes on, however, a brief word is necessary concerning what this book is about and who it is for.

It is primarily a book for those who are curious, confused, dissatisfied, hurt or struggling with sexuality, and who want some answers. For all the promises of the sexual revolution, many are now realizing that the last 30 years have not produced the joyous sexual utopia that was hoped for. Could it be that there are other answers that actually make sense of our sexuality, and allow us to express and enjoy it? This book suggests that there are.

While we will spend quite some pages looking at the Bible, and at what God says in it about sex, this is by no means a book just for Christian believers or 'religious' people. It is for Christians, certainly–and we trust that it will be of some help, especially for those who are at the age where issues of sex and marriage are foremost in the mind. However, it is just as much a book for those who might sit rather loose to Christian teaching or church, and yet who remain disturbed at where society is heading, or at where their own lives are heading. It is a book for those who feel hurt and used, and also for those who feel a residual pang for having used others. We should warn you: it is a book that may make you feel worse before it makes you feel any better.

Most of all, we hope it will be a book that tells the truth, as uncomfortable as it might sometimes be, for only the truth, in the end, can set us free.

Phillip Jensen & Tony Payne
JUNE, 1998

CHAPTER 1

The queer, the unhappy and the irrelevant

Many say that the *Sydney Morning Herald* is not the fine broadsheet it once was, but for capturing the mood of our time it still has few equals. Take three articles which recently appeared close by one another in the first six pages of the Saturday 'Spectrum' section[1]. A better summary of the prevailing sexual climate would be hard to find.

First there is an article entitled "Queer, really queer" about developments in cutting edge gay and lesbian theatre. 'Queer', as the genre of performance is called, is a growing movement at "the artistic frontier, where perversity, pain and pornography reign". It's a "powerful and empowering sensibility" that goes well beyond the narrow confines of the term 'gay'. It's an exciting form of performance art, mixing dance, theatre, cabaret, pornography, circus, shamanism, sex work and sado-masochism. Queer

1. November 8, 1997.

artists like per.ver.city, Vyl, Miss Fit, Trash Vaudeville and The Bum Puppets, do everything and anything on stage, claiming to offer "plenty of laughs and something to offend everyone". Accordingly, their audiences often find themselves splattered with faeces and vomit. And lest we think that this form of entertainment is the preserve of a small, marginalized sub-culture, the article trumpets the fact that Queer is gaining acceptance at a wider level, and is beginning the journey towards mainstream, as evidenced by recent Australia Council and Arts Council of Great Britain funding for its projects.

It seems we've come a long way from the days of Queen Victoria, who declined to legislate against lesbianism because she refused to believe that such a thing existed. Here is sex at its most 'free', even if the freedom involves whips and chains.

It must also be pointed out that we have come a long way in just the last 35 years. Many readers of the *Sydney Morning Herald* in 1962 would, like Queen Victoria, have found it hard to imagine that such practices existed. Now the *Herald* not only tells us of their existence, but breathlessly promotes them.

This very liberal attitude to sexuality is part of the air we breath, and many readers of this book may have grown up knowing little else. The sexual revolution of the last 35 years or so has profoundly changed Western attitudes and behaviour towards sex. Although statistics on sexual behaviour are often open to question, there is overwhelming evidence of massive changes in both the way we act and think regarding sex. The frequency of premarital sex amongst teenagers, for example, exploded in the period following the 1960s. Depending on whose figures one uses, the percentage of girls under the age of 16 who experienced premarital intercourse was around 5% in the early 1950s. By 1973, it was 30%. Throughout the rest of the 70s and 80s, the trend continued.[2] By 1989, 59% of all American high-schoolers professed to having engaged in premarital sex.[3]

It is not only behaviour that has changed. Our attitudes have also undergone a revolution. In 1965, 69% of American women and 65% of men under 30 said that premarital sex was always or almost always wrong. Just seven years later in 1972, those figures had dropped to 24% and 21% respectively.[4] By 1990, in Britain, the comparable figure was down to 6%.

Much the same trend can be seen in social attitudes to previously taboo or frowned upon practices like divorce, cohabitation, births out of wedlock and homosexuality. These are now widely considered to be merely alternative lifestyle choices.

Over the past 35 years, our society has undertaken

---

2. Figures from various studies cited in Marita P. McCabe, "Sexual attitudes and behaviour in Australian adolescents", in D. T. Kenny & R. F. Soames Job (eds), *Australia's Adolescents: a health psychology perspective* (Armidale: UNE Press, 1995), p. 197. These figures need to be treated with some caution, as do most statistics related to this area. While they can be indicative of trends, it is hard to achieve accuracy, especially when like is often not being compared with like.
3. Figures from the Centers for Disease Control, cited by Frederica Matthewes-Green, "Now for some good news", *First Things*, No. 75, Aug/Sep 1997, p. 20.
4. Cited in G. Himmelfarb, *The De-Moralization of Society*, (New York: Alfred Knopf, 1995) p. 236.

a quest for pure sex–sex unadulterated and free, stripped of all the guilt, repression and uptight restrictions of the 50s. Many regard it as a revolution that was long overdue, and there is little doubt that it succeeded. Sex is now out of the closet and comfortably sitting in the family armchair. In fact, sex is everywhere, selling every product, spicing every movie, changing every relationship. Prime-time television now has programs which discuss (and illustrate) the advantages of certain sex positions, and the best way to achieve multiple orgasms.

With increased sexual freedom has come increased sexual problems, and some are beginning to question whether the revolution has gone too far, or even whether it was such a great idea in the first place.

Which brings us to the second *Herald* article. In "Unhappily Ever After", Bettina Arndt, one of Australia's best-known sexologists and for many years an outspoken advocate of sexual freedom, writes of a growing body of evidence concerning marriage and divorce. Her opening paragraphs are worth quoting at length:

> Staying together for the sake of the kids. It's such an outdated notion. What was once seen as an act of sacrifice and moral strength is today dismissed as misguided masochism. Bitter tight-lipped martyrs living in hell with their equally miserable kids. Who needs it?
>
> For the past two or three decades, we have embraced a different approach to the issue of children and marriage breakdown: namely, that divorce is better for kids than growing up with

> parents in a troubled marriage. Parents who take care of themselves will be best able to take care of their children...
>
> It is a notion that has met with wide public support, as social institutions joined in the joyful celebration of family diversity. Who could forget the Year of the Family, when we witnessed strenuous efforts to downplay any advantage traditional families could offer children? The idea of family has become all-embracing, with all relationships, all living arrangements, held as equally valuable.
>
> But now the ground is shifting. In the past few years, the evidence has become overwhelming that divorce is having detrimental effects on the lives of many Australian children. Abundant research, here and abroad, demonstrates that the intact two-parent family offers children distinct and life-lasting advantages over single-parent and blended families.

Arndt goes on to show not only that the evidence is overwhelming, but that those studies that purported to show otherwise were poorly constructed and interpreted. She even quotes a family crisis worker as saying that those who run our social institutions are ignoring the problem for their own personal reasons: "A lot of the people who set the social agenda and work in the media in this country are middle-class intellectuals living the lifestyles we are talking about. They do not want to address these issues because it makes them personally uncomfortable."

Even such bastions of liberal thought as *The Atlantic Monthly* are joining the current mood of sexual disquiet. Barbara Defoe Whitehead's article "Dan Quayle was right" caused a storm when it was published in 1993. She demonstrates (at great length) that Western society's headlong rush into divorce, single-parenting and blended families has been an unmitigated social disaster, especially for the children. On every possible indicator, the children of divorce do substantially worse than children in intact, two-parent families, even when those families are suffering conflict and stress. Although she has no desire to admit it (as a staunch Democrat), Whitehead says that Dan Quayle was right when he so famously criticised TV character Murphy Brown for glorifying single motherhood.

Whitehead argues that in the last generation, Americans have embraced a 'culture of divorce', in which divorce and family breakup is seen as a natural and even desirable form of personal renewal. Family breakup has been depicted as "a drama of revolution and rebirth. The nuclear family represents the corrupt past, an institution guilty of the abuse of power and the suppression of individual freedom...Liberated from the bonds of the family, the individual can achieve independence and experience a new beginning, a fresh start, a new birth of freedom."

This spirit of personal freedom and rebellion against conventional constraint is at the heart of the sexual revolution. It is no accident that growth in promiscuity and all forms of sexual expression since the 60s was matched by a similar explosion in divorce. What is now being recognized with increasing dismay is that this impulse has actually resulted in enormous personal and social damage.

Arndt and Whitehead aren't the only ones making grumbling noises along these lines. Younger feminists like Naomi Wolf are also questioning the orthodoxies of abortion on demand and sexual promiscuity, and have earned the wrath of other feminists for their trouble.[5]

Nor is dissent from the revolution only being found among the ranks of the intellectuals and opinion-shapers. There is also evidence that teenagers are starting to work out that sexual liberation may not always be as liberating as everybody says. For the first time since the 60s, there has actually been a *drop* in the promiscuity of teenagers, according to recent research in America. From the high point of 1989, where 59% of high schoolers had engaged in sex, the figure dropped slightly in 1990 to 54%. It was 43% in 1992. In 1994, the Roper Organization released a study which claimed that only 36% of high schoolers had had sex.[6]

---

5. "Naomi the big bad Wolf?" in *The Sydney Morning Herald*, 17/10/95 reports how a recent *New Republic* article by Wolf caused a stir in feminist circles. Having recently married and had a baby, Wolf now believes that a woman who has an abortion without facing the moral dilemmas has "fallen short of who she should be". Wolf goes on to warn: "We stand in danger of losing what can only be called our souls". The *Herald* article accuses her of pontificating and selling out to the pro-life lobby. Wolf's most recent book *Promiscuities* (Chatto & Windus, 1997) also raised the ire of critics by questioning the wisdom of 60s and 70s style sexual freedom.

6. Cited by Frederica Matthewes-Green, op. cit., p. 20.

Even if these figures are only broadly accurate, they reflect a shift in attitudes. Numerous factors might account for it, the arrival of AIDS no doubt being one. However, could it also be that girls especially are realizing that sexual freedom may also include the freedom to say No. If the traditional view has any validity that 'boys offer love to get sex, and girls offer sex to get love', who loses when the value of sex goes down? With the price of sex at an all time low, are girls getting sick of having to dole out huge quantities just to buy a little affection?

There is a deep and growing sense in many sections of our society that we haven't got it right about sex. There is more sexual 'freedom', in the sense that very few avenues are now closed, but few would testify that it has resulted in better relationships–only in a greater quantity of broken and dissatisfying relationships. We have more sex than ever before (or at least say we do), but we also have more sex and relationship counsellors than ever before. Many reading this book will doubtless know personally of the hurt, confusion and quiet despair that comes from broken relationships, made only more painful by the sexual dimension of that relationship.

Where might we turn for answers in this confusing environment? To 'the church' perhaps?

The third of the *Herald* articles demonstrates just how unlikely that might be. It is entitled "God Smacked", and concerns the intrigue and political machinations afflicting a small Congregational Church in Sydney's Balmain. The picture that emerges is a classic stereotype of Christianity as many modern people see it. The minister is the Rev Frederick Lambert-Carter, a kindly old man in a white robe who actually starred as the minister in the Whiskas cat-food commercial of the early 90s, and who supplements his income by staging picturesque wedding ceremonies for honeymooning Japanese couples. The small congregation is at each other's throats over the issue of whether it is now time for the very elderly Rev Lambeth-Carter to retire, and who should succeed him–especially since the church pulls in nearly $300,000 a year in revenue from the weekly Balmain markets that take place in the church grounds, and has property assets worth several million dollars.[7]

Here is a picture of late twentieth century Christianity–small in number, marginalized, and squabbling over the wealth they have from the assets of a bygone era. In a word, irrelevant.

In these three articles, placed at random (one would assume) in a mainstream daily newspaper, we have a concise picture of the late twentieth century sexual landscape. Rampant promiscuity, disturbing voices of disquiet and dissatisfaction, and the church as a spent force.

In light of this, it might well be asked: Why then are Christians, of all people, writing a book on 'pure sex'? Not only is Christianity now on the margins, but what does it stand for? Wasn't it Christianity that gave us the uptight, repressive, Victorian hypocrisy that we have left behind? Don't Christians see sex as naughty or distasteful, and only to be endured for the sake of begetting children? Were they not the pathetic voices on the sidelines during the 60s and 70s, offering a lame and futile protest

---

7. The Rev. Lambeth-Carter has subsequently resigned his post amidst ongoing acrimony.

while we freed ourselves from the dead hand of sexual repression, taboo and the double standard? What have Christians got to say about sex except "Don't"?

From the tone of that caricature, the reader can doubtless work out that we would like to differentiate ourselves from the kind of cardboard Christian that is so often mocked (or ignored) in our popular culture. We regard biblical Christianity as being far from irrelevant to the sexual dilemmas of Western culture, and we hope that by the end of this book our readers might agree.

One thing we will certainly not be doing is simply listing and defending a series of moral virtues, or offering a new set of commandments for the 21st century. This is rather too much like treating the symptoms, while leaving the disease undiagnosed, and ultimately untreated.

Nor will we be exploring in any detail the many (often contradictory) things that Christians have said about sex over the past 2000 years–for the simple reason that the rightness or wrongness of those views can only be measured by going back to the definitive and authoritative document of Christianity: the Bible. In due course, we will look at its basic teaching regarding sex, before thinking further about about how this relates to the complex world of sexuality that confronts us.

However, even this basic step of reading the Bible and seeing what it actually says–as opposed to the stereotype–may bring its share of surprises. The Bible is a powerful and threatening book. It has a way of reading us, even as we read it. As C. H. Spurgeon so famously said of the Bible: "There is no need for you to defend a lion when he is being attacked. All you need to do is to open the gate and let him out!"

CHAPTER 2

The search for nudity

In Erica Jong's feminist novel about sex, *Fear of Flying*, the main character embarks on a quest for the perfect sexual experience. She wants ultimate sex, free from all the emotional garbage and repression that seem to ruin most sexual encounters and relationships. And she bed-hops her way through life in search of it.

This is a parable for the modern world. We want sex to be great, to be free, to be uninhibited and joyous. Yet, like Erica Jong's character, most of us find the pursuit of this sort of sex elusive. A progression of one-night stands or casual relationships doesn't seem to do it. Indeed, the impersonal nature of casual sex, which at one level lends it a certain mystique and excitement, at another level offers diminishing returns. It is hard to sustain the open, uninhibited self-giving which makes for really satisfying sex when the other person is a stranger to you, and may or may not be there in the morning.

Nor does an ever more daring search for new sexual boundaries to cross yield the rewards of excitement and pleasure that are sometimes promised. In a satirical piece on the growing fashionability of bisexuality, Julie Burchill puts it like this:

> In the case of sexuality, as Bagehot famously said of the monarchy, it does not do to let too much daylight in upon enchantment. Too much permission can paradoxically have the effect on an individual and a society's eroticism which repression can only dream of. The Victorians only succeeded in making sex seem even dirtier (and therefore more desirable) with their chintzy chadors thrown frenziedly over everything from women to dining tables and their Here Be Dragons attitude to the act itself; but show me a swamp full of naked hippies playing hide-the-Frisbee at some 60s Love The One You're With festival, and I'll show you something guaranteed to put you off your sexual feed...quicker than a dose of bromide in your All-Bran...[1]

Which leads us to ask: How do we hope that our lives will be better because of sex? Is it a case of simply accumulating orgasms, and the one who has had the most when he dies wins? Or is there more to it than that? What do we really want from sex?

It could just be that the answer is nudity.

Is it possible that what we really want is a relationship not simply of physical nakedness and pleasure, but of deep personal nakedness as well? A partner before

---

1. Julie Burchill, "Sex and sensibility with an each way bet", *The Good Weekend* (*Sydney Morning Herald* magazine), April 13, 1996.

whom we can be totally open; someone who can accept us and love us and desire us as we are; a relationship of honesty and love, where satisfying sex springs not only from a deep acceptance of each other, but an ongoing desire to please the other person. Is not this what we dream of? We long for a situation in which we are completely at one with another person, and where each partner is as much (or more) concerned with the other person's pleasure as their own, where the excitement and pleasure the other person is receiving gives us pleasure as well. Each one serving and pleasuring the other; each one worshipping the other's body. We would want this sort of relationship to go on for a long time, and to grow in intimacy and mutual pleasure, as each learns how to please the other even more.

The strange thing is that the Bible–that black-leather bound book which is usually regarded as anti-sex, or at best barely tolerant of it–espouses just this vision of sexuality. In the ancient texts of Christianity, there is a view of sex that is gloriously optimistic and inspiring, and yet at the same time very down-to-earth and realistic. It is a view that has much to attract us, and yet which also may seem strange to us at some points, so different is it from the attitudes and values that dominate our culture.

In this chapter, we will try briefly to clear away some of the misconceptions and myths, and outline in basic terms what these biblical writings from two millennia (and more) ago have to say about sex.

Nudity in the Garden

As we turn to the opening chapters of Genesis, we read of the creation of the world, of humanity and of sex. In particular, we find that God creates sexuality with some clear *purposes* in mind. This in itself is a somewhat foreign idea to the modern mind–the suggestion that sex might have a purpose, that it may have been designed to achieve certain things, to serve as the means to certain ends, rather than simply being an end in itself. In Genesis, human sexuality has two purposes.

The first comes out in Genesis 1. In this chapter, the purpose of male/female sexuality is *to produce children.* The man and woman are blessed by God and commanded to multiply and fill the earth.

In our sexual climate, children are an unfortunate by-product of sex, to be avoided on most occasions. Thanks to effective contraception, modern Western society has severed the age-old link between sex and children. One no longer necessarily follows the other.

However, the modern ideal of keeping the number of children to an acceptable minimum–or avoiding them altogether–is an idea that the biblical writers would have regarded as perverse. They were familiar of course with childless marriages, but they regarded them as a great sadness, and as a reason for fervent prayer that God might 'open the womb' of the unfortunate woman. They saw children not as an inconvenience, but as a blessing from God.

This attitude stems from the biblical understanding of life, in which *relationships* are the most real and important things that exist. The formation of family units–of grandparents and parents and children and aunts and uncles–allows us constantly to enjoy a network of relationships, to love and be loved, to give ourselves to others. This is how we were created to be.

However, sex is not only about making babies (although some Christians in history taught otherwise). We need to notice that Genesis outlines a second and equally important purpose of sex: *a deep personal union between a man and a woman.* In Genesis 2, God makes the woman as a companion for the man, someone with whom he can enjoy union and relationship. She is different from him, but in that very difference lies the potential for a profound unity between the two. And sex plays an important part in this.

> The man said, "This is now bone of my bones and flesh of my flesh; she shall be called 'woman', for she was taken out of man". For this reason a man will leave his father and mother and be united to his wife, and they will become one flesh. The man and his wife were both naked, and they felt no shame (Genesis 2:23-25).

This passage should dispel forever the myth that God is anti-sex, or that sex is somehow part of our 'lower' animal natures. In the paradise of Eden, before they sinned, God creates man and woman as sexual beings, who enjoy sexual union as the natural, healthy expression of their naked, married intimacy. Having left their parents, and set up home together, the man and woman become one, domestically, emotionally and physically. Sex is the physical bond that unites them. It is the glue of their unity, which they enjoy without fear or shame.

In the garden, God creates sex as a profound interpersonal act between the man and the woman. It is not a casual or neutral bodily function, like shaking hands or going to the toilet. It is an act of the deepest personal intimacy and self-giving. If it is working properly, sex bonds us to the other person. We become not only physically one with them, but deeply emotionally one with them as well. And once a sexual relationship has begun, it cannot be ended without grief.

The immense power of sex is quite apparent in divorce. No matter how unhappy the marriage, in the first two years following separation or divorce, people usually experience what some counsellors call the 'normal crazies'. They become slightly unhinged–nervous, lacking in confidence, having to rediscover themselves as persons. Even though the marriage may have been a disaster, the separation is still deeply hurtful. Sexuality is a strong adhesive. It binds us to the other person, and when we are separated from them, we feel torn apart.

However, let us not to be negative. The Bible portrays the bonding power of sex as a precious gift from God. It unites a man and woman in a bond of mutual intimacy and pleasure. It builds and cements the relationship, and helps repair it when it is damaged. It should be enjoyed and practised often.

God created sexuality with these two purposes in mind: to produce children, and to build deep personal unity between a man and a woman. The Bible records God's own assessment of his creative work: "God saw all that he had made, and it was very good" (Genesis 1:31).

Sex *is* very good, and by this we mean not simply that it feels good (although it does most of the time) but that it achieves very good things–that is, when it is used properly.

God's framework for sex

If these are the twin purposes of sex, the context or situation God establishes for sex makes perfect sense: lifelong, monogamous marriage. One man, one woman, united for life. This is the context in which children can be produced and nurtured, and in which the uniting, bonding power of sex can really do its work.

The goodness and rightness of this framework can be seen by a consideration of the alternatives. To have children outside the stability of a permanent monogamous relationship is cruel to the child, as well as to the mother, who usually bears the burden of raising and supporting the child in the absence of a permanent father. And to bond ourselves to someone sexually outside the permanency of a marriage relationship is also damaging, for both parties. It creates wounds that others can't see, but which touch the core of our personalities. When the break up occurs, we are torn apart. And with each successive episode, we become less capable of giving ourselves to another, and enjoying the free and intimate union with another person that sex was designed to facilitate.

God's framework for sex springs from what sex is for and how it works. It is not an arbitrary set of rules, as if God wanted to test us, or as if he didn't want us to enjoy ourselves too much. Far from it. Because God created sex, he understands its nature and power, and what it is for—and thus he designates a permanent, committed, exclusive relationship as the place in which sex is to take place. It is like the warning printed on the plastic bags in which children's toys come: "Please dispose of this bag after opening. This bag is not a toy." The plastic *can* be used as a toy, especially for the game that all children love of putting it over their heads, and waiting to turn blue. But that's not what the bag is for, and to use it that way is disastrous.

Sex is not a toy. And as the Bible unfolds, God places various limits on the practice of sex. These limits all stem from the basic idea that God created sex a particular way, for particular purposes. To violate those purposes is to misuse sex, and is therefore both wrong and ultimately harmful. It goes against the basic structures and order of creation. The restrictions are not arbitrary, or in some sense merely 'cultural'. They reflect the wisdom of the Creator.

Beyond Genesis

Both of these themes–the goodness of sex, and the importance of using it within God's framework–are reflected (and further expounded) throughout the rest of the Bible.

The Law of Moses, for example, has a reputation in popular culture for being simply a long list of 'thou shalt nots', and for being very negative and restrictive about all things sexual. This is a caricature. The teaching of the Law on sex builds on what we have seen in Genesis. It assumes that sex is a good part of God's creation, and that the Israelites must express their sexuality in certain ways (and not in other ways).

At one level, we find instructions like this for newlyweds:

> If a man has recently married, he must not be sent to war or have any other duty laid on him. For one year he is to be free to stay at home and bring happiness to the wife he has married (Deuteronomy 24:5).

This law expresses the goodness of marriage and sex, but also the importance of newlyweds taking time to build their relationship–including the sexual aspect of it–right from the outset.[2]

We also find numerous laws and instructions detailing how the Israelites were to show themselves different from the surrounding nations by expressing their sexuality only within God's framework of marriage. Thus, Israel was not to commit adultery, as the Seventh Commandment said (see Exodus 20:14; Deuteronomy 5:18; Levitcus 20:10). Adultery was a denial of God's purposes for sex and marriage, a basic act of betrayal and faithlessness, punishable by the extreme penalty.

Adultery was not the only sexual pattern forbidden to the Israelites. They were not to commit incest (Leviticus 18:1-18), nor to practise homosexual[3] acts or bestiality (Leviticus 18:22, 23). These practices were abhorrent to God, because they transgressed the basic created structures of sexuality.

Adultery and the fool

The book of Proverbs also urges its readers to respect the created framework for sex, but from a slightly different angle–from the 'common sense' viewpoint that, in practical terms, stepping outside God's framework leads

---

2. It is also quite possible that the phrase 'bring happiness to his wife' in this context may refer to giving her children; or indeed that the sexual enjoyment and production of children were so closely tied together in the author's mind that both ideas are caught up in the phrase.
3. For more on homosexuality, see Appendix I.

to disaster. Adultery is the prime example. The adulterer is not simply doing the wrong thing, according to Proverbs; he is also a fool.

> A man who commits adultery lacks judgment; whoever does so destroys himself. Blows and disgrace are his lot, and his shame will never be wiped away; for jealousy arouses a husband's fury, and he will show no mercy when he takes revenge. He will not accept any compensation; he will refuse the bribe, however great it is (Proverbs 6:32-35).

Adultery is to be avoided at all costs. It appears to be the path into excitement, sexual intrigue, and enjoyment. But it is the path to destruction. In a complete reversal of our society's values, Proverbs sees adultery as far worse than prostitution:

> Do not lust in your heart after her [the adulteress's] beauty or let her captivate you with her eyes, for the prostitute reduces you to a loaf of bread, but the adulteress preys upon your very life (Proverbs 6:25-26).

In both prostitution and adultery there is a payment to be made, but only in adultery is that payment one's very life.

However, Proverbs also encourages its readers to enjoy the pleasures of sex. In chapter 5, following a warning about adultery, Solomon urges his son to delight in the sexual favours of his wife:

> Drink water from your own cistern[4], running water from your own well. Should your springs overflow in the streets, your streams of water in the public squares? Let them be yours alone, never to be shared with strangers. May your fountain be blessed, and may you rejoice in the wife of your youth. A loving doe, a graceful deer–may her breasts satisfy you always, may you ever be captivated by her love. Why be captivated, my son, by an adulteress? Why embrace the bosom of another man's wife? (Proverbs 5:15-20).

This is a striking passage, and not only because it compares one's wife to a water tank! Solomon is quite frank about it: Don't destroy yourself with adultery, when you can have pure sex at home with your wife. Delight yourself in her, he instructs. Enjoy the pleasure of her breasts. Be captivated by her love.

This is not the language of the sexually repressed. It expresses both the realism and idealism of the Bible–that sex is a normal part of life to be talked about frankly, and yet also that sex is a very significant activity; it is not a neutral physical act to be practised with just anyone.

This is not the only passage in Proverbs to extol the virtues of marriage. Among others, there is the saying in Proverbs 18:22–"He who finds a wife finds what is good and receives favour from the LORD"–as well as the long passage in Proverbs 31 about the wife of noble character.

---

4. This is referring to a water storage tank, not part of a toilet.

In Proverbs, as in the Bible as a whole, sex is regarded as a delightful part of God's creation, a good gift to be received and enjoyed. Yet because of its powerful effects, and the disastrous consequences of misusing it, sex is also to be treated with care and respect.

The Bible's sealed section

These two aspects of sexuality–its pleasures and its dangers–are powerfully expressed in the most sexually charged book of the whole Bible: Song of Songs.

Whatever else this love poem may mean (and there has been much discussion on this in Christian history), it clearly celebrates the beauty and goodness of sexual love. The lovers are intoxicated with each other, and their passion is described in imagery that is as beautiful as it is erotic:

> Your two breasts are like two fawns, like twin fawns of a gazelle that browse among the lilies. Until the day breaks and the shadows flee, I will go to the mountain of myrrh and to the hill of incense. All beautiful you are, my darling; there is no flaw in you (Song of Songs 4:5-7).
>
> How beautiful you are and how pleasing, O love, with your delights! Your stature is like that of the palm, and your breasts like clusters of fruit. I said, "I will climb the palm tree; I will take hold of its fruit." May your breasts be like the clusters of the vine, the fragrance of your breath like apples, and your mouth like the best wine.
>
> May the wine go straight to my lover, flowing gently over lips and teeth (Song of Songs 7:6-9).

For all the beauty and joy of love in the Song of Songs, the book also reflects the dangers and complexities of our desires. The relationship between the Shulammite and Solomon is an illicit one, conducted in secret, with all the intrigue of night-time meetings, lingering good-byes and agonized longings. It is a clandestine affair, with the woman even preferring that her lover was like a brother to her, so that she could embrace and kiss him openly without being despised (8:1). It is in some sense a forbidden love, and hence the woman's constant refrain:

> Daughters of Jerusalem, I charge you by the gazelles and by the does of the field: Do not arouse or awaken love until it so desires (Song of Songs 2:7; also 3:5; 8:4).

The message of the book seems to be this: that while love and sex between a man and woman is a wonderful thing, it should nevertheless take place within a certain sphere. There is a right time and place for love to be awakened and aroused. Love is powerful. It is as "strong as death, its jealousy unyielding as the grave" (8:6). Once it is unleashed, there is no turning back, and the consequences are unavoidable.

In the context of the whole Bible's story, it is hardly surprising that Solomon is identified as the male lover in the poem. For in Solomon, that most wise and majestic of kings, we see all that is good in Israel, and yet also all that is tragic. Solomon's sexual appetite was his undoing. His many foreign wives turned his heart away from God. He, more than anyone in the Old Testament, epitomises what happens when the beauty of sex is not kept within the framework God has created.

Jesus and sex

As we turn from the Old Testament to the New, we find Jesus reinforcing the basic teaching of Genesis 1-2 regarding sex and marriage:

> Some Pharisees came to him to test him. They asked, "Is it lawful for a man to divorce his wife for any and every reason?"
>
> "Haven't you read," he replied, "that at the beginning the Creator made them male and female', and said, 'For this reason a man will leave his father and mother and be united to his wife, and the two will become one flesh'? So they are no longer two, but one. Therefore what God has joined together, let man not separate" (Matthew 19:3-6).

We do not have room at this point to discuss the complexities of divorce and remarriage, but one thing is obvious, namely that Jesus endorses the vision of Genesis 1-2, and regards it as applicable to divorce. As far as Jesus is concerned, God created man and woman for lifelong unity in marriage.

The rest of the New Testament has a similar perspective. Marriage is an excellent thing, to be honoured by all (Hebrews 13:4). Indeed, to forbid marriage, as if celibacy were somehow more spiritual or holy, is a "doctrine taught by demons" according to 1 Timothy 4. 1 Corinthians 7 also puts forward a very positive view of sex, with marriage as its framework, and husbands and wives enjoying its pleasures–and often.

> The husband should fulfil his marital duty to his wife, and likewise the wife to her husband. The wife's body does not belong to her alone but also to her husband. In the same way, the husband's body does not belong to him alone but also to his wife. Do not deprive each other except by mutual consent and for a time, so that you may devote yourselves to prayer. Then come together again so that Satan will not tempt you because of your lack of self-control (1 Corinthians 7:3-5).

The wife's body belongs to her husband, for the satisfaction of his sexual needs. If this sounds like chauvinistic slavery, notice that the reverse also applies: the husband's body belongs to his wife. The two of them are mutually enslaved for the sake of the other's sexual needs. It was not *Cleo* or *Cosmopolitan*, or Germaine Greer for that matter, who discovered that women have sexual needs. It's been there in the Bible all along.

A view from another planet

This then, in basic terms, is the biblical view of sex. There is more to be said, but we cannot proceed any further without dealing with the obvious fact that the view we have begun to outline is in stark contrast to our prevailing culture. There are parts of what we have been outlining that many people would endorse, such as the fundamental goodness of sex, its powerful effects, and the desirability of having sex within a loving relationship. However, there is much else that seems to us anachronistic and out of date–such as the notion that sex belongs only in marriage, or that a key purpose of sex is having children.

These sorts of views are so far removed from the dominant attitudes and values of our time that if we were inclined to accept them, and implement them, we would find ourselves acting as counter-cultural radicals, even revolutionaries. Not only so, we would need to conduct a revolution in our own thinking. We have absorbed the sexual attitudes and values of our society from childhood, with every magazine, with every film, with every TV show, and in every classroom.

In fact, those who have been born since 1960 may not even be aware of how profoundly our society's attitudes and behaviour have changed over the past 35 years or so. We take it for granted that sex should not be restricted to marriage, that adultery is a normal fact of life, that widespread and frequent divorce is necessary and unavoidable, and that homosexuality is a very common and perfectly valid lifestyle choice. It is hard for us to conceive of a world in which these attitudes were not dominant. But that world was our own society little more than a generation ago.

The sexual revolution of the last 35 years or so has wrought enormous changes in attitudes and practice, and it is simply not possible to proceed any further in our thinking about sex without confronting this reality. How did our society come to undergo such profound changes? Why did we have a sexual revolution? What, exactly, was our society revolting against?

CHAPTER 3

A brief history of sex

Why did we have a sexual revolution?

Did a bunch of 60s hippies get together one night and decide it was time for a change? Or were the 50s so bad that no-one could stand it anymore?

Given that human beings have always found sex alluring and attractive, why was it in the 60s (and the decades following) that Western society threw off the shackles and leapt into bed with each other. What happened?

This is a very important question. If we are to understand the current sexual landscape, and how we might navigate our way through it, we need to look back. We need to understand how we got here. What were the forces, people and events that gave rise to such a dramatic change in sexual attitudes and behaviour?

At one level, the generation who were arriving into young adulthood in the 60s was ripe for revolution. They were a generation who had never known a world war or the social upheavals of economic depression. They had grown up in the prosperous 50s, and entered the 60s in huge numbers, and at an age of sexual growth and awakening. They were the 'baby boomers', and if any generation was ready to throw themselves enthusiastically into a sexual revolution it was they.

To a significant extent, the revolution was the result of new technology–the ready availability of the contraceptive pill. Now, for the first time in human history, the link between sexual intercourse and child-bearing could simply and effectively be broken. The possibility of pregnancy, with all its social and practical drawbacks, was no longer part of the equation. The Pill made promiscuity an apparently risk-free business.

A more relaxed attitude to sex was now not only deliciously possible (in practical terms), but was becoming socially more acceptable. It was a time when traditional structures and morality were being openly questioned. Church attendance and religious observance generally were on the decline. The 23-year prime ministership of Sir Robert Menzies, who stood as a symbol of the conservatism and moral rectitude of the 50s, came to an end in 1965–although some would say it didn't really end until the election of Gough Whitlam in 1972. The writings of early feminists like Betty Friedan and Germaine Greer criticised the sexual double-standard, whereby it was acceptable for young men to 'sow their wild oats' but not for young women. It was the age of the Beatles, of 'making love not war', of hippies and pot and rock'n'roll.

These sorts of factors have often been pointed to as 'causes' of the sexual revolution, or at least as the fertile soil in which it rapidly grew.[1] While there is little doubt

---

1. See McCabe, op. cit., for a standard summary.

that these factors all played their part, if we are to understand what happened, and how things came to be as they are, we need to go much further back. To change metaphors, the 60s might have been when the explosion took place, but the fuse had been lit long before.

In this chapter (and the next), we will try to understand who lit that fuse and when. It will be a brief history, and necessarily a simplified one–more of a 'highlights package' than a full account, and by no means the final word. Nevertheless, the point will be obvious enough, and for those who want to chase these ideas further, there is guidance in the footnotes.

Our journey begins around a century ago. If we are to understand the first thing about modern sexuality, and why it changed so much so quickly, we must go back to our much-maligned ancestors, the Victorians.

The naughtiness of piano legs

Literally speaking, a 'Victorian' is someone who lived during the long reign of Queen Victoria, from 1837-1901. The term has come to mean, however, far more than this. It now refers to an attitude or stance towards morality and convention, which is regarded as being typical of England in the latter half of the nineteenth century. To us, a 'Victorian' set of values (or 'virtues' as they would have put it), is one that is hopelessly outdated, rigid, formal and hung-up. It refers to a repressed, stiff-upper lip form of moral rectitude, in which one must always behave 'properly', morally and with good manners, at least in public. In particular, to be Victorian is to have a repressed and hypocritical attitude towards sex–to make covers for the legs of pianos because of the immoral connotations and suggestions that a bare, curvaceous leg might have on the minds of the easily corruptible; and yet at the same time, to keep a private mistress to satisfy one's sexual appetites. A facade of public respectability and sexual strictness, with a cauldron of suppressed sexuality and immorality lurking beneath.

This stereotype of 'Victorian' morality is rather too simplistic, and owes much to the famously caustic biographies of Lytton Strachey. Strachey had his own reasons for ridiculing Victorian morality, which we will see in due course. It is even doubtful that the famous practice of covering piano-legs ever actually occurred.[2]

However, whatever simplifications or overstatements might be made, there is a kernel of truth in this depiction of the Victorian era. In a series of works which have received justifiable critical acclaim, historian Gertrude Himmelfarb has shown that morality was a big issue for the Victorians, not because of religious faith, but because of the *loss* of religious faith:

> When [George] Eliot was asked how morality could subsist in the absence of religious faith, she replied that God was "inconceivable", immortality "unbelievable" and Duty nonetheless "peremptory and absolute". This is the clue to the Victorian obsession with morality. Feeling guilty about the loss of their religious faith, suspecting that that loss might expose them to the temptations of immorality and the perils of nihilism...

---

2. Gertrude Himmelfarb, *Marriage and Morals among the Victorians* (London: Faber and Faber, 1986), pp. 15-16, note 16.

> they were determined to make of morality a substitute for religion–to make of it, indeed, a form of religion. And having forfeited the sanctions of religion, they were thrown back all the more on the sanctions of convention and law.[3]

Among the writers, poets, artists and intellectuals of the Victorian age, belief in biblical Christianity was steadily receding. The days of the evangelical revival and the height of Methodism were becoming a distant memory. As Matthew Arnold so famously put it:

> The Sea of Faith
> Was once, too, at the full, and round earth's
> shore
> Lay like the fold of a bright girdle furled.
> But now I only hear
> Its melancholy, long, withdrawing roar,
> Retreating, to the breath
> Of the night-wind, down the vast edges drear
> And naked shingles of the world.[4]

The causes of this loss of faith are complex, but its reality was undeniable. What the Victorians did not come to terms with was that without God, morality could not be sustained for long by the forces of convention and law alone. They clung resolutely to the *content* of Christian morality, for they feared the consequences of abandoning it. In the generation that followed, however, there was no such fear.

---

3. *ibid.*, p. 21.
4. Dover Beach.

The Bloomsbury set

As the new century dawned, the children of the Victorians had no qualms about throwing off what they saw as a set of stifling moral conventions. The name most immediately associated with the new era of freedom was Bloomsbury, taken from the London district where Virginia Stephen (later Woolf) took up residence with her brother and sister. They became the heart of a close-knit group of artists and intellectuals who sought moral and spiritual liberation from the strictures of Victorianism.

Their basic philosophy of life, which they drew from the philosopher G. E. Moore, was to pursue higher 'states of consciousness', through human relationships and the enjoyment of beautiful objects.[5] It was a philosophy that deliberately rejected conventional morality, and lived for the good of present experience, repudiating duty, convention, law and programmes of moral improvement or social action.

The Bloomsbury group were seen as radicals, but a more influential group of radicals could scarcely be found. Members and associates of Bloomsbury were prominent in the fields of art, literature and intellectual endeavour–people such as the biographer Lytton Strachey, the artists Duncan Grant, Roger Fry and Clive Bell, the novelists Virginia Woolf and E. M. Forster, and the economist John Maynard Keynes. It was following the trail blazed by Bloomsbury that the promiscuous

---

5. Whether the Bloomsbury group actually based their ideals on Moore's work, or found in it a coherent and convenient expression of what they already believed is open to question.

'Bohemian' culture flourished in the 1920s, and likewise the Sydney Push of the 1950s and 60s. As Himmelfarb points out, these movements were still at the radical margins of the society rather than at its everyday core, yet they were no less visible, and influential, for being so.

In the words of Leonard Woolf (Virginia's husband) the Bloomsbury group saw themselves as "the builders of a new society which should be free, rational, civilized", and many since have praised their wit and fidelity, their pursuit of truth and good sense, their close-knit and affectionate relationships, free of the constraints of Victorian guilt and shame.[6]

The logic of their position was certainly hard to shake. If God was dead, as Nietzsche had said, and as a growing number of turn-of-the-century intellectuals believed, then what hold could morals and convention have over the liberated mind? What else should one pursue except the pleasures of love and sex and sensual beauty that the Victorians had so needlessly repressed?

It's all about sex

The word 'repressed' leads us naturally to another major player in the recent history of sex, the founder of psychoanalysis, Sigmund Freud. Forests have been pulped in describing and analysing Freud's work, which was complex and evolved considerably during his lifetime. It is difficult to know how to do justice to it in this short space.

In basic terms, Freud sought an explanation for human behaviour, and in particular neurotic illnesses

---

6. A survey of the literature is found in Himmelfarb, op. cit., p. 45-6.

and problems, in the functions of the human unconscious. Freud believed that the human mind was like a mechanical system into which energy flowed. This 'energy' was largely sexual, and how the system dealt with this energy–whether it diverted it, blocked it, expressed it, repressed it, or whatever–determined to a large degree the mental health of the individual.

Without going into the intricacies, Freud saw sex as the basic determinant of who we are, and what we become. More than any intellectual before him, Freud talked openly and frankly about sex, in a way which startled his contemporaries. It was not so much that Freud advocated free love, or any vast social change in sexual mores. "But in the matter of expression and speech his attitude was completely revolutionary. In this way he shocked alike those who viewed sex as very sacred and those who viewed it as indecent."[7]

In the wake of Freud, sex was not only a topic for discussion; it was now a potentially dangerous force in the human psyche, if it was not dealt with properly. In popular terms, Freudianism was taken to teach that if sexual instincts were repressed or in some way not allowed their natural expression, neurotic illness was the likely outcome. After Freud, the family was no longer seen as the place of protection, nurture and the teaching of 'good morals'; it was a constricting, unhealthy place, in which crippling attitudes to sexuality lead to various damaging psychological complexes.

---

7. Havelock Ellis, "Freud's influence on the changed attitude to sex", *American Journal of Sociology*, 45/3, Nov 1939, p. 313.

Sex comes of age

Freud was not the only one to suggest that conventional 'morality' may be unhealthy, or unnecessary. The idea that sexual values and morals were merely expressions of a particular culture, and were not innate or universal, was championed by the American anthropologist Margaret Mead. Her best-selling book *Coming of Age in Samoa*, published in 1928, was claimed to be based on extensive field research, and demonstrated that sexual conventions and experiences in Samoa were vastly different than in, for example, America.

In particular, Mead argued that the adolescents of Samoa engaged in free sexual experimentation and promiscuity, without guilt or other harmful effects, and that their society was a model of contentment and happiness. Samoans, Mead argued,

> ...laugh at stories of romantic love, scoff at fidelity to a long absent wife or mistress, believe explicitly that one love will cure another... Adultery does not necessarily mean a broken marriage... Divorce is a simple informal matter... It is a very brittle monogamy often trespassed and more often broken entirely, but many adulteries occur...which hardly threaten the continuity of established relationships..., and so there are no marriages of any duration in which either person is actively unhappy.[8]

---

8. Margaret Mead, *Coming of Age in Samoa: A Psychological Study of Primitive Youth for Western Civilization* (New York: Blue Ribbon Books, 1928), p. 104-8.

In short, Mead portrayed Samoa as a paradise of uninhibited sexual free love. Not surprisingly perhaps, Mead's ideas met with an enthusiastic reception. She became a media and academic superstar, roles Mead herself did not resist. She was vigorous in popularizing her research, and the lessons that it contained for Western culture. Her basic contention–that nurture not nature accounts for taboos and restrictions on sexuality–has been enormously influential throughout the latter half of our century.

The pursuit of tolerance and kindness

If Margaret Mead argued for sexual liberation from the viewpoint of anthropology, another leading intellectual argued for it on the basis of philosophy. Bertrand Russell was one of our century's most famous philosophers and atheists, and argued that the superstition of religion did great harm when it came to sex. In fact, Russell regarded Christianity's "morbid and unnatural" attitude towards sex as its worst feature.[9]

He argued that monogamy as an institution was on its last legs in the Western world. The forces that held it together were all on the wane–the social narrowness of village life; the superstitions of religion, sin and eternal punishment; and the sanction of public opinion. For

---

9. Bertrand Russell, "Has Religion made useful contributions to civilization?" in *Why I am not a Christian* (London: Unwin, 1957), p. 29. Russell's views on sexuality are summarized in another essay in this same collection, entitled "Our Sexual Ethics", written in 1936.

Russell, there was no higher or divine law of good and bad, only actions which do or do not promote human happiness.

It was upon this basis (which philosophically is called 'utilitarianism') that a 'sexual ethic' should be worked out, although as to what this would mean in practice Russell was a little less clear. He certainly wished there to be a greater degree of sexual freedom to individuals, especially for young people, before the advent of children complicated the termination of the relationship. But Russell also acknowledged that the contradictory impulses of jealousy and polygamy–which he regarded as basic to human experience–made the formulation of a satisfactory modern code of sexual behaviour far from simple.

In the end, like any good utilitarian, Russell favoured a 'wait and see' approach to evaluate what results the changing conventions of sex yielded.[10] "In the meantime", he concludes, "it would be well if men and women could remember, in sexual relationship, in marriage, and in divorce, to practise the ordinary virtues of tolerance, kindness, truthfulness, and justice".

These are words we will come back to.

---

10. As many have pointed out, this is one of the problems with utilitarianism. Not only is it notoriously difficult to define what constitutes 'happiness' for people, as well as to justify why 'happiness' should be the defining characteristic, it is also hard to say when the experiment should stop. How long should we wait and see, and how will we measure the quantity of 'happiness' when the time comes? We will return to this point in chapter 6.

Everybody's doing it

Our final stop on this brief historical journey is in America in the late 1940s. It was there that a respectable 53-year-old former entomologist (his specialty was the gall wasp) published a fat scientific study that *Life* magazine declared to be the most sensational and popular scientific work published since Darwin's *Origin of the Species.* The work was entitled *Sexual Behaviour in the Human Male*, and its author was Dr Alfred Kinsey.

The Kinsey Report, as it came to be known, was revolutionary, not simply because of its size and comprehensiveness, but because it lifted the lid on sexual taboos and behaviour that Americans had previously been reluctant to discuss. Kinsey (and his co-authors Pomeroy and Martin) surveyed a massive sample of Americans and reported that 90 per cent of males masturbated, 85% had engaged in premarital intercourse, 30-45% had conducted extra-marital sexual relationships, and around 70% had visited prostitutes. Furthermore, Kinsey contended that 37% of males had experienced homosexual orgasm post-puberty, that 10% of the population were predominantly homosexual and 4% exclusively so.

The implications of Kinsey's research were not lost on the American public. If, for example, 10% of the population were homosexual (which was how the figures were popularly represented), then homosexuality was no longer a deviant criminal act ('sodomy') only practised by a very small number of social outcasts. It ought now to be recognized as the fairly common behaviour of a large minority. Many homosexual activists cite Kinsey as the man who made the modern gay movement possible.[11]

The same could be said of masturbation or pre- or extra-marital sex. If these were as normal as Kinsey had found, then perhaps it was time to leave behind the stifling conventions of respectable middle-class life, and accept openly what was obviously happening anyway. After Kinsey, the conversation about sex was on a new level. As a step towards the overthrowing of conventional moral norms, it was a defining moment.

A slow-burning fuse

As this brief history has tried to demonstrate, the sexual revolution of the last 30 years has been a long time in the making. The abandonment of conventional or 'Victorian' sexual morality that occurred among the Bloomsbury group prefigured what was to happen on a mass scale later in the century. It was there, perhaps, that the fuse was lit. Freud, Mead, Russell and Kinsey all played their part (and, of course, they were not the only ones). They kept it burning, as it were, and laid the explosive. It was in the mid-60s, when the conditions were right, that the bomb went off.

What must be remembered, however, is that lying behind the whole process was *a previous generation's rejection of God.* The late-Victorians lived on the moral capital of their forefathers. Their loss of faith may have rendered their morals formal, sterile and ultimately

---

11. See Mark Thompson (ed), *The Long Road to Freedom* (New York: St Martin's Press, 1994), p. 22, 59-60, 102, 164, cited in J. Reisman, "Kinsey and the Homosexual Revolution" in George A. Rekers (ed), *The Journal of Human Sexuality* (Carollton: Lewis and Stanley, 1996), p. 21.

hypocritical, but the sense of duty and morality remained, such was the residual power of the religion of the parents' generation. But by the next generation, there was no such constraining force. When Bloomsbury looked at the late Victorians, all they could see was morality and good manners being kept for the sake of convention. They could see no logical barrier to the moral and sexual liberation they eagerly sought.

It took much of the rest of the century for this logic to filter down through society as a whole. Society's 'gatekeepers'–the intellectuals, university teachers, commentators, journalists, film-makers–played an important role in this 'percolation' process, and an examination of that role would make an interesting study (but one which we do not have time for here[12]).

Nevertheless, the sexual attitudes and behaviour that are now commonplace and accepted in our society can only be understood in light of the historical background we have been outlining in this chapter–or should we say, the *theological* background. The sexual revolution was not simply a rebellion against traditional morality; it was the consequence of a rebellion against God, who defined the terms of that morality.

We may not be used to thinking this way, but this is partly because Western society's rejection of Christianity is now so longstanding. We now take for granted that sexual promiscuity is natural, and that it is even harmful

---

12. Michael Medved's book, *Hollywood vs. America* (New York: HarperPerennial, 1992) is a fascinating example of one such study.

to repress it (thanks to Freud et al). We assume that the taboos and conventions of traditional sexual morality are simply constructs of our culture, and therefore can be changed or ignored as we wish (thanks to Bloomsbury, Mead and the rest). We find it hard to think that particular sexual acts are 'wrong'–they are just the personal preference of particular people, and may be far more common than you think (thanks to Kinsey et al).

All of these assumptions are the consequence of first dispensing with God. And, historically speaking, that is precisely what occurred. At the level of intellectual debate, God and Christianity have been under severe attack since the middle of the 19th century.

In fact, a curious and ironic reversal has taken place. Now, at the end of the 20th century, it is the dominant secular society which seeks to impose its sexual values on the marginalized minority of Christians–for example, in berating churches for not marrying practising homosexuals.

Our society has, as a whole, cast off the 'irrational superstitions of Christian dogma'. Following instead the path of 'free intellectual and scientific research', we have now supposedly arrived at a more enlightened and liberated stance towards sexuality. And for this we can thank pioneers like Bloomsbury, Freud, Mead, Russell and Kinsey.

But not all is as it seems.

CHAPTER 4

The heart has its reasons

When Woody Allen faced the media, and sought to explain his sexual relationship with the adopted teenage daughter of his wife Mia Farrow, he eventually shrugged his shoulders and said, "The heart wants what it wants".

This, it seems, was justification enough. And while the popular media tut-tutted about the scandal, it was hard-pressed to find any compelling reason to condemn Allen's behaviour. After all, it is the same message as a thousand Hollywood movies and popular novels. We must follow our heart, and if what our heart wants happens to be illicit, forbidden or condemned by 'conventional morality', then so much the worse for conventional morality.

Whether he was doing so consciously or not, Woody Allen was echoing a more famous quotation from the French philosopher Pascal: "The heart has its reasons which the mind knows nothing of".

This is a truth that has been long recognized. Human beings are frequently unaware of their own motives, or only dimly aware of them. We pursue a particular course of action, often for reasons we can't articulate, and only afterwards do we think about it, and try to come up with some sort of justification for what we have done. These after-thoughts are often referred to as 'rationalizing' our behaviour.

Although Freud has been roundly criticised in recent times, he was surely right in recognizing the truth of this at least. Our attitudes and thinking do have a complex relationship with our behaviour. At one level, we act in a certain way because we believe certain things to be true; however, we also come to believe certain things to be true *because of how we live*, and what we have done. Our behaviour and desires affect our thinking. Our intellectual life is profoundly influenced by our moral life (as the Bible has always taught).

This is particularly true as we think about sex, because sex is such a powerful and basic desire within our personalities. Is it possible to think clearly and rationally about sex without our own desires intruding? Can we conduct an inquiry into sexuality without our own personal sexual histories quietly contributing to the shape of our conclusions?

Dirty linen and dodgy science

Lytton Strachey, that prominent member of the Bloomsbury group, wrote what has been called the first 'modern biography'–*Eminent Victorians*, in which he ridiculed famous Victorians for their hypocrisy and repressed sexuality. Rather than simply record the heroic achievements of his subjects, Strachey sought to go behind the respectable Victorian facade and expose the damning truth of their private immorality. It is ironic that the very kind of biography that Strachey pioneered should now have exposed so much of his own private life, and those of his friends.

It is only through a spate of biographies published in the last 30 years, that the extraordinary and compulsive promiscuity of Bloomsbury has become known. Theirs was by no means a disinterested search for enlightenment, beauty and truth. Their intellectual advocacy of a departure from Victorian conventions and restrictions took place in an atmosphere of sexual (and homosexual) promiscuity, the extent of which even the participants marvelled at. In 1907, Strachey discovered that his homosexual lover (and cousin) Duncan Grant was simultaneously having an affair with Arthur Hobhouse, who in turn was having an affair with John Maynard Keynes. Within a year, Strachey was also disturbed to discover that Grant and Keynes were now lovers as well. He wrote to Leonard Woolf: "Dieu! It's a mad mixture; are you shocked? We do rather permeate and combine. I've never been in love with Maynard and I've never copulated with Hobbes [Hobhouse], but at the moment I can't think of any more exceptions."[1]

Nor was the sexual intrigue only of the homosexual variety. Vanessa Stephen was married to Clive Bell, but while Clive was having a series of affairs with Molly McCarthy, Vanessa began a sexual relationship with

1. Cited in Himmelfarb, *Marriage and Morals*, p. 43-4. The movie *Carrington* portrays something of Strachey's extreme licentiousness and the pain that it caused, but true to the spirit of our age contrives to put a sympathetic gloss upon it.

Roger Fry, which lasted two years until Vanessa began to transfer her affections to (the at least temporarily heterosexual) Duncan Grant, who had been the lover of Strachey, Keynes and Vanessa's brother Adrian. Angelica, Vanessa's child by Duncan, eventually married David ('Bunny') Garrett, who was 26 years her senior, and had been at one time Duncan's lover.

Gertrude Himmelfarb aptly describes the sexual atmosphere of Bloomsbury as "not only homosexual but androgynous, near-incestuous, and polymorphously promiscuous". If their exploits had been known at the time, or even in the decades following, perhaps historians and commentators would not have been so quick to characterize Bloomsbury as embodying "a life of rational and pacific freedom" or of "reason, charity and good sense".[2]

Did Bloomsbury pursue this lifestyle of astonishing promiscuity because they had coolly decided that it was the logical way to create the good society based on reason, charity and good sense? Or did the sexual possibilities that rejection of God would open up have more than a passing influence on their judgement?

Much the same pattern can be seen amongst the other pioneers of modern sexuality. In each case, it has now become clear that personal factors, especially sexual preferences and practices, had an enormous influence on the development of their theories, and a correspondingly detrimental effect on the quality of their research.

In Freud's case, the origins and driving forces behind his now largely discredited theories have been the subject

---

2. *ibid*, p. 45.

of numerous recent studies.[3] Was it his obsessive need for intellectual fame that led him to devise such an extravagant theory, and to portray himself in messianic terms as the hero-saviour of humanity? Or was it his affair with his wife's sister, Minna Bernays, that drove him to construct a psychological theory to explain why all of us are supposedly motivated to commit incest?

Many of Freud's theories are such that they are impossible either to prove or disprove, dealing as they do in the realm of assertions, impressions and interpretations. The same cannot be said, however, for Margaret Mead. It is now well known that her Samoan research was deeply flawed, and that some of her key informants did not tell her the truth. As Australian anthropologist Derek Freeman has shown, the real Samoa was very far removed from Mead's paradise of free love. It was, in fact, a society with strict sexual conventions, which jealously guarded the virginity of young girls, and severely punished adultery. Against Mead's contention that "the idea of forceful rape or of any sexual act to which the participants do not give themselves freely is completely foreign to the Samoan mind", Freeman demonstrated from police records that the rate of rape in Samoa was actually one of the highest to be found anywhere in the world.[4]

---

3. For a coolly argued and devastating recent critique, see Richard Webster, *Why Freud was wrong* (London: Fontana, 1996).
4. See Derek Freeman, *Margaret Mead and Samoa: The Making and Unmaking of an Anthropological Myth* (Cambridge, Mass: Harvard University Press, 1983). For a fuller discussion of the Mead/Freeman controversy, see Phillip D. Jensen, "Margaret Mead, Derek Freeman and intellectual leadership" in *kategoria* 1996, number 2, pp. 9-22.

It is not difficult to see why Mead's portrait of Samoa received such a favourable reception. It sent all the right messages to a society which was keen to dispense with the rigid norms of morality, and to live the free, uninhibited, sexual life which the island paradise of Samoa seemed to typify. The only problem was that the research on which Mead based her sweeping conclusions was almost entirely false. As E. Michael Jones puts it: "*Coming of Age in Samoa*, that idyll of casual sex beneath the palm trees, was proving to be about as scientific as the screenplay of *Blue Lagoon*".[5]

Jones goes on to point out that it is not hard to find disturbing undercurrents in Mead's own personal life that explain her extraordinary misinterpretation of Samoan society. At the time she was preparing to embark for Samoa in 1925, Mead (who had then been married for about two years) was conducting an adulterous relationship with the linguist Edward Sapir, as well as a lesbian affair with her mentor in anthropology, Ruth Benedict.[6] That she had strong personal motivation to overthrow conventional morality is undeniable, and there seems little doubt that this significantly influenced her research and conclusions. Even her friend and academic ally Lowell Holmes was forced to admit: "I think it is quite true that Margaret finds pretty much what she wants to find".[7]

---

5. E. Michael Jones, *Degenerate Moderns: Modernity as Rationalized Sexual Misbehavior* (San Francisco: Ignatius, 1993), p. 33.
6. As recorded in the memoir written by Mead's daughter (from her third marriage), Mary Catherine Bateson, cited in Jones, *ibid*, p. 35.
7. In a letter to Derek Freeman, again cited in Jones, *ibid*, p. 30.

Bertrand Russell was a supporter of Mead, and a close associate of the Bloomsbury group, and in their work found support for his own utilitarian sexual ethic. However, Russell, too, was not developing his philosophy in an atmosphere of detached speculation. In fact, as Ray Monk's recent massive biography makes plain, Russell's life was characterized by a long series of adulterous affairs conducted with an extraordinary degree of selfishness, deceit and cruelty.[8]

In providing a very detailed account of Russell's life, with its many hypocrisies and deceptions, Monk frankly acknowledges: "I am aware that the personality thus revealed is one that many will find repellent, but it has not been my aim to present him in an unfavourable light". Whatever Monk's aim, the end result certainly makes good sense of Russell's desire to relax the bonds of sexual convention. What is harder to reconcile is how the

---

8. Ray Monk, *Bertrand Russell: The Spirit of Solitude* (London: Jonathan Cape, 1996). Russell's treatment of a young American woman, Helen Dudley, provides just one characteristic example of his behaviour. Having met Miss Dudley in America, Russell suggested she come back to England to live with him and eventually marry, if he could secure a divorce from his wife Alys. At the same time, he told another lover, Ottoline Morrell (the wife of a close friend), that he had slept with Helen only out of philanthropy, to foster her creativity as a writer. Ottoline was not happy about this, and after a few days back in England, Russell concluded that his relationship with Helen was not so serious after all. When the unfortunate Helen arrived in England to take up Russell's invitation, he refused even to see her. Helen ended up in a mental asylum. Monk goes on to show that Russell's own account of the affair in his autobiography is totally hypocritical. See Monk, p. 356f.

personality revealed in Monk's biography could have stated in such high-sounding tones that "it would be well if men and women could remember, in sexual relationship, in marriage, and in divorce, to practise the ordinary virtues of tolerance, kindness, truthfulness, and justice".

When we come to Alfred Kinsey, the pattern is sadly the same. It is now clear that Kinsey himself was a homosexual, and a masochist (in the sexual sense) who, as he grew older, pursued an interest in extreme forms of sexuality, with an increasing compulsiveness.[9] At the time of his famous report, Kinsey had begun conducting (and participating in) sexual experiments in his attic, filming members of his staff having sex with each other, and with his wife, and also filming exhibitions of gay sex, especially of the sado-masochistic variety.

Kinsey, there seems little doubt, had powerful personal reasons for pursuing sex research, and for attempting to demonstrate that there was no such thing as 'deviancy'. Not surprisingly, as with Mead, personal bias led Kinsey to scientific sleight-of-hand, if not outright fraud. The details of Kinsey's work have since been seriously undermined. Judith Reisman is one of a number of recent critics who argue that Kinsey's research was both fraudulent and criminal.[10] His sample of American males, although large, was hardly represen-

---

9. This is the verdict of Kinsey's most recent biographer, James H. Jones, writing for *The Australian Magazine*, Nov 22-23, 1997. His biography is entitled, *Alfred C. Kinsey: A Public/Private Life*, published by Norton, 1997.
10. Reisman, *op cit.*

tative of the population as a whole. 26% of Kinsey's subjects, for example, were 'sex offenders'; a further 25% were in prison; among the rest, pimps, male prostitutes and frequenters of 'gay bars' were over-represented. There is little doubt that sexually promiscuous males, especially homosexuals, were massively over-represented in Kinsey's sample, but this is something that Kinsey repeatedly denied or attempted to obscure. Thus Kinsey's contention that 10% of the population is predominantly homosexual is a massive exaggeration. A barrage of more recent studies have put the figure at around 1% for men, and less than half that for women–and this after 30 years of gay activism to make being homosexual a socially acceptable lifestyle.[11]

Moreover, alarming questions have been raised (and not answered) about the methods of Kinsey's research into pre-adolescent orgasm. The Kinsey Report contains detailed statistics on the nature of orgasms among 929 male subjects, ranging in age from 5 months to 14 years of age. The tables of statistics speak of "speed of pre-adolescent orgasm; duration of stimulation before climax; observations timed with second hand or stop watch". The question of course is: *How were these figures obtained?* How was Kinsey able to report, for example, on the 10 year-old boy who had 14 orgasms in a 24 hour

---

11. For a summary of these studies see Andrew Shead "Homosexuality and the church: history of the debate" in B. G. Webb (ed), *Theological and Pastoral Responses to Homosexuality (Explorations 8),* (Adelaide: Openbook, 1994). Also see, J. Dallas, "Responding to Pro-Gay Theology" in G. R. Rekers (ed), *The Journal of Human Sexuality* (Carollton: Lewis and Stanley, 1996), p. 79.

period, or the 4 year-old subject who was able to be stimulated to 26 orgasms in a 24-hour period, or the 11 month old who had 14 orgasms in 38 minutes?

Reisman provides evidence that Kinsey recruited and trained paedophiles to conduct this research on his behalf, and that their contact with the children concerned sometimes took place over months and even years.

The more that becomes known about Kinsey, and about the details of his research, the more alarming is the fact that his Report was a central plank in the modern argument for sexual liberation.

God and sex?

The more we investigate the background to the sexual revolution, and thus to the prevailing sexual climate today, the more complex the picture becomes. At one level, it is quite clear that the widespread abandonment of Christian belief gave Victorian morality its particular shape, and paved the way for its rejection in the generations to follow. The story of twentieth century sexual morality is the story of a society gradually working out the implications of God no longer being in the picture.

Yet the rejection of God and the eventual widespread acceptance of sexual liberation are not quite so simply related to each other as that. For which came first? A rejection of God leading to sexual promiscuity? Or a desire for promiscuity leading to a rejection of the God who would condemn such promiscuity? Or are the two so closely tied together it is impossible to say?

One thing can be said–the steadily growing argument for sexual liberation, conducted throughout the twentieth century by the likes of Bloomsbury, Freud,

Mead and Kinsey, now looks increasingly like a hurriedly stitched together covering of fig-leaves to hide a lost innocence.

And this takes our mind back to another revolution, the first and most important of all, and the prototype of all that would follow. For the Victorian rebellion against God, and all the consequences that flowed from it, are an apt illustration–or rather imitation–of the first rebellion. The rebellion of Adam and Eve.

CHAPTER 5

A failed revolution

She has no clothes on. Her nakedness is only covered by her astonishingly long blonde hair which somehow manages to keep the relevant bits from view. She holds a rich red apple in her hand. Slowly she takes a bite, and then turns to camera and says huskily, "Be tempted".

We have seen this ad a thousand times. It can be used to sell everything from Tasmania to sheep drench. It works because most people, however little they know about the Bible or Christianity, still know something about Adam and Eve, and the apple. And somehow the whole thing has to do with sex.

As is so often the case, the facts and the stereotype have parted company somewhere along the line. Many modern people reject the story of Adam and Eve as a repressive, reactionary myth about why sex is naughty. But when we open the pages of Genesis and read the account for ourselves, a couple of things are quite clear. Firstly, whatever Adam and Eve did wrong, it had nothing to do with sex. As we have already seen, sex was part of God's good creation. Before the serpent, before the sin, before any of the mess that followed, Adam and Eve were enjoying the 'one flesh' sexual union that God had created them for. Eve wasn't a blonde temptress who sinfully seduced Adam into having sex with her. She was his wife (blonde or otherwise).

Secondly, there was no apple. The tree which they eventually ate from wasn't an apple tree, or for that matter an orange tree. It was "the tree of the knowledge of good and evil" (Genesis 2:16-17). It was the one tree that God had forbidden them to eat from, with the warning that "when you eat of it you will surely die".

When the temptation comes, through the wily suggestions of the serpent, it attacks Eve's powers of resistance on several fronts. She is tempted to doubt both the reality of God's warning, and the goodness of his motives. "You will not surely die", says the serpent. "For God knows that when you eat of it your eyes will be opened, and you will be like God, knowing good and evil." The implication is clear–God is simply protecting his own position. He wants to keep humanity in submission, to tyrannize them. The delicious prospect placed before Eve by the serpent is that she herself will become like God, and that there will be no repercussions.

On top of all this, the fruit itself is a "delight to the eyes". And so she eats. She gives some to her husband and he eats as well. The essence of it is *rebellion.* They begin to doubt God, and whether he really has their best interests at heart. They decide that they don't want God to tell them what to do. And so they attempt to become like God themselves, to usurp his wisdom and power.

The consequence is disaster. Humanity's rebellion

against God affects not only their relationship with God, but with each other. It is one of the myths of modern society that 'spirituality' or 'religion' is one's own business, a private matter. This is patently untrue. The commitments and decisions you make about God will shape the kind of person you are, and that person is the one that others will have to deal with in society.

In fact, rejection of God will always be anti-social in the end, for the very essence of rejecting God's rule over our lives is the establishment of *our* rule over our lives. We are all spiritual separatists. We want to reject God's government, and set up our own. We want autonomy. We want to be our own little gods, ruling our own little worlds. This may work quite well–that is, until you come and stand too close to me. For you, too, are your own little god. And there is never room for two gods in the world. If we both want to have control over the part of the world we share, then there will be warfare. Rejection of God is fundamentally self-centred. And self-centred people find it hard to get along with other self-centred people.

This is pictured in Adam and Eve. The naked intimacy of chapter 2 gives way to fear and hiding in chapter 3. In the rebellious world of the Fall, the man looks at the woman, and the woman looks at the man, and both work out very quickly what each can do to the other. It is no longer a free world of open relationship and harmony. They must hide themselves, not only from God, but from each other. And so, rather pathetically, they sew for themselves a covering of fig-leaves.

God confirms and reinforces the consequences of their having rejected him. It they wish to make up their own rules, then such it will be, but the harmony that they previously enjoyed (with God and each other and the whole creation) will no longer hold.

In fact, God's judgement of Adam and Eve for their rebellion fits the crime. The woman was created for fellowship with the man, to be his mate, and the bearer of their children. It is in this sphere, as wife and child-bearer, that she is judged. Childbearing becomes much more painful, and the intimate husband-wife union of chapter 2 is replaced by conflict. Similarly, the man's work of tending the fruitful and bounteous garden is replaced by the toil and sweat of frustrating work, with the ground no longer being so cooperative.

The chapter ends with humanity expelled from Eden, and facing the grim consequences of being separated from God. They face death, and a world which is now tainted and distorted. The Fall will effect every aspect of their existence, including sex. Sex was not the sin of Adam and Eve, but their rebellion against God results in a distortion and corruption of sex.

The perversion is the punishment

In popular mythology, it is assumed that sex is the ultimate sin (and therefore the one that Adam and Eve committed) and results in God's judgement. However, the Bible's viewpoint is almost exactly the opposite of this. It is not that sex is sinful–far from it. The essence of sin is rebelling against God, and once we do this, all of life, including sex, becomes distorted. In fact, the distortion of sex, and the degrading of our personalities that follows, is *part of God's judgement on us.*

This is taught in Romans 1:18-32, which outlines

both the character of sin and of judgement.

In verses 18-23, we see the essence of sin:

> The wrath of God is being revealed from heaven against all the godlessness and wickedness of men who suppress the truth by their wickedness, since what may be known about God is plain to them, because God has made it plain to them. For since the creation of the world God's invisible qualities–his eternal power and divine nature–have been clearly seen, being understood from what has been made, so that men are without excuse. For although they knew God, they neither glorified him as God nor gave thanks to him, but their thinking became futile and their foolish hearts were darkened. Although they claimed to be wise, they became fools and exchanged the glory of the immortal God for images made to look like mortal man and birds and animals and reptiles (Romans 1:18-23).

People know of God's eternal power and divine nature, yet suppress this knowledge and live a lie. They base their lives on the falsehood that God is *not* the eternally powerful creator. Though they claim to be wise, they end up foolishly worshipping created things, which are far less than God.

God's response is to 'give them over' to the consequences of their folly. Notice how this solemn phrase is repeated three times in the paragraphs that follow:

> Therefore *God gave them over* in the sinful desires of their hearts to sexual impurity for the degrad-

> ing of their bodies with one another. They exchanged the truth of God for a lie, and worshipped and served created things rather than the Creator–who is for ever praised. Amen.
>
> Because of this, *God gave them over* to shameful lusts. Even their women exchanged natural relations for unnatural ones. In the same way the men also abandoned natural relations with women and were inflamed with lust for one another. Men committed indecent acts with other men, and received in themselves the due penalty for their perversion.
>
> Furthermore, since they did not think it worth while to retain the knowledge of God, *he gave them over* to a depraved mind, to do what ought not to be done. They have become filled with every kind of wickedness, evil, greed and depravity. They are full of envy, murder, strife, deceit and malice. They are gossips, slanderers, God-haters, insolent, arrogant and boastful; they invent ways of doing evil; they disobey their parents; they are senseless, faithless, heartless, ruthless. Although they know God's righteous decree that those who do such things deserve death, they not only continue to do these very things but also approve of those who practise them (Romans 1:24-32).

This is a picture of our world, with no sugar-coating. The Bible is such a realistic book. It deals with realities of fornication, incest, homosexual practices and rape, because that's the way the world was and is. Indeed, in our society, it is beginning to become apparent just how many children have been abused by step-fathers and others in positions of trust. Having rejected God, we have constructed a perverse and destructive lifestyle.

God is rightly angry that we reject him and worship the created things rather than the Creator. And his anger is expressed in allowing us to go our own way, and to suffer the degrading consequences. Sinful and distorted sexuality is part of this. It is the very fitting punishment that God has given us over to. In cutting ourselves off from him, the Creator of all good things (including sex), we find ourselves lost in a tangle of perverse and degrading behaviour.

This perspective is so utterly foreign to our normal way of thinking that it needs to be made quite clear. When we see sexual immorality of any kind, we not only see people sinning, but also people under the judgement of God. The behaviour they are engaged in is perverse. It is not how relationships were created to work. It lowers our dignity as God's creation. The sexual sin that people get caught in, and indeed revel in, is a sign of disaster. It is an indicator that we are under God's condemnation for our rebellion against him, and his good order for the world.

When we see something beautiful and good being defiled or degraded it can make us quite furious. And so it should. From God's perspective, this is just how we should see sexual sin. It is the shameful perversion of a good and beautiful thing. It is something to be appalled at.

This, of course, is not how we see it. We see illicit sex as glamorous, exciting, titillating and captivating. We see it as the ultimate in human freedom and enjoyment. Christians even sometimes find themselves envying their non-Christian neighbours in their sexual 'freedom'.

But there is nothing to envy. Sexual immorality is not only a punishment in itself, but it has destructive consequences, both socially and personally. And increasingly, even those who once were at the forefront, advocating the so-called glories and freedoms of the sexual revolution, now realise that the consequences have not at all been what they hoped for.

The strange case of Richard Neville

In 1972, Richard Neville had just emerged triumphant from the longest obscenity trial in British history. First in Australia, and then in London, Neville had been at the editorial centre of *Oz*, an alternative, anti-establishment magazine which sought to shock, satirize, and generally make hay in the increasingly liberated sunshine of the late 60s. *Oz* set out to break the rules, and in particular the rules of censorship.

If *Oz*, and Richard Neville, stood for anything, it was the right to publish anything in the name of free speech. Even if society at large regarded *Oz* as obscene, pornographic and blasphemous, that was no reason to deny it the free right to express and distribute its views in whatever manner it saw fit. They were heady days, and the *Oz* trial made Richard Neville a celebrity. It was one of the defining moments in the censorship debate, in which the advocates of liberation argued for a relaxation of the draconian and repressive laws of the past.

Censorship was always fought out on the basis of whether one particular product would corrupt the society, and this is why the anti-censorship argument was so powerful. The publication of one book like *Lady Chatterley's Lover* manifestly won't make much difference to a whole society.[1] But over time, a difference will be made, as a drop of water will wear away a rock, with many drops over many years. One obscene publication or play may not make much difference, but when every second magazine, TV, film or play presents a particular view of morality (or amorality), then it does affect the way we think, and this affects the way we act.

As a case study in the liberation of sexual attitudes, the progress of the censorship debate is worth noting. The very people who argued so forcibly in the 60s for 'anything goes' are now protesting just as vociferously at the degrading, dehumanizing, perverse material that is shown in the modern media. 25 years down the track, Richard Neville is now dismayed at the vicious, violent, appalling material that is paraded as 'art' in the works of film-maker Peter Greenaway. He put it like this:

> Our generation has spent its formative years fighting for freedom of expression. We had trials, demos, and alternative press, pirate radio, sit-ins, the burning of bras and the unbanning of books. An era which began with the liberation of *Lady Chatterley's Lover* went on to canonize the Sex Pistols. Perhaps it's because we put so much energy into the defence of freedom that it goes against the grain to pass judgement on anything obnoxious, especially if it is deft, daring or unusual.[2]

---

1. D. H. Lawrence's erotic novel of illicit love was acquitted of obscenity charges in a celebrated trial in London in 1960.
2. Richard Neville, *Out of my mind* (Penguin, 1996), p. 76.

Neville goes on to argue, however, that pass judgement we must. We can no longer smile and subject ourselves to the mental and emotional garbage that is heaped upon us. In describing Greenaway's film *The cook, the thief, his wife and her lover*, Neville's judgement is as follows:

> ...What we are left with is this–a load of the same substance that was smeared on the nude in the beginning (human excrement)–with a difference. Unlike the victim, viewers do not have the benefit of a hose-down...
>
> Sure let's clean up the garbage in Antarctica, but what of the garbage in our living-rooms? This is not to seek a revival of censorship, imposed from the top, but to renounce our reticence for what it is–a hangover from a long-lost era of uptightness.
>
> Stage, TV, cinema, books and magazines–what is their impact on society; and how do they influence our values and attitudes? Is their message reflective, as so many claim, or can they foster pestilence? [3]

Neville clearly thinks that the media can foster pestilence, arguing that there is evidence that *American Psycho* by Brett Easton Ellis played a role in the Strathfield massacre, in which Wade Frankum went on a killing spree in a suburban Sydney shopping mall.

Neville fears that we as a culture are deeply vulnerable to how the media can influence us, and he laments

3. *ibid*, p. 78.

that some of his baby-boomer friends are reluctant to acknowledge this:

> Those whose views were crystallized in the censorship wars of the sixties decry the possibility that the prolonged and excessive depiction of hideous events in the media could have a detrimental social effect. Nor do they connect this cultural pathology with our ailing environment.[4]

However, Neville now has no such doubts. He is certain that the proliferation of exploitative porn and splatter-trash is ruining our society. "It's time to tackle a system which fouls another resource–the river of our dreams, our desires and our collective destiny."

By any standards, this is an astonishing back-flip. In the late 60s, Neville thought little of treading on the sensibilities of others. Now, 25 years later, with his own sensibilities being given a beating, he wants something done about it. Exactly what, he is not sure.

What Neville is struggling to come to terms with is something that the Bible is very clear on–namely, that sin is not only an offence against God. It is also anti-social and anti-self.

The destructive consequences

By its very nature, sexual immorality is *anti-social*. Just as you cannot love your neighbour and steal from him at the same time, so you cannot love him and commit adultery with his wife (see Romans 13:8-10). "Love does

---

4. *ibid*, p. 155.

no harm to its neighbour", and is therefore a summary of all the commandments. Sexual immorality, like all disobedience to God's command, is a failure to love. It not only does harm to our neighbour, but very often to a wider circle of people as well.

When one partner in a marriage runs off with someone else, it is not just the partner left behind who is devastated. The children also suffer long-term effects, including loss of self-esteem, behaviour problems and so on. The wider circle of family is also affected, with grandparents, in particular, often being deeply hurt by being cut off from their grandchildren.

Sexual immorality, such as adultery, is profoundly destructive. And when a society has abandoned itself to it, as ours has, the effects are disastrous. We will be living with them for generations to come.

Sexual immorality is also *anti-self*. It is a crime against our own persons. In this sense, sexual sins *are* worse than other sins (although we will see below that in another sense they are not!). The Bible puts it this way:

> Flee from sexual immorality. All other sins a man commits are outside his body, but he who sins sexually sins against his own body. Do you not know that your body is a temple of the Holy Spirit, who is in you, whom you have received from God? You are not your own; you were bought at a price. Therefore honour God with your body. (1 Corinthians 6:18-20).

Sexual immorality defiles our bodies, which (if we are Christians) are temples of God's Holy Spirit. Our bodies are unique and precious, for they are the possession, and dwelling place, of God himself, in the person of his Spirit.

Therefore, sexual sins are different. They are sins undertaken with our bodies, and which therefore corrupt and damage us, and dishonour the God who created and redeemed us.

The consequences of sexual sin are serious and long-lasting. If we steal from the tax man by understating our income, we have sinned. And if we are caught, we will have to pay the price, not only in terms of making restitution, but in terms of the humiliation and punishment. However, once the debt is paid, and the wrong put right, the subsequent consequences can be dealt with. It is a sin external to me.

However, what we do with and to our bodies is what we do with and to our very selves. We are never the same again. We may be forgiven; we may try to make it up; but we are still different. Our self-identity and self-worth are affected by sex. We cannot detach ourselves from our bodies, and from what we do with our bodies. This is why sexual immorality has such a capacity for devastating people.

This devastation is being experienced across all levels in our society. At one level, it can be seen in statistics relating to adultery, divorce, the effects of divorce on children, the incidence of sexually transmitted diseases (AIDS being only one of these), the rate of illegitimacy, and so on. However, the cost is also born personally and privately in a way that statistics will never reveal, but which many readers of this book will doubtless be able to confirm. The hurt that results from being psychologically manipulated or used in a sexual relationship is massive. It leaves scars that make the next relationship that much harder to sustain.

In its consequences for ourselves and for others, few other sins are as damaging as sexual immorality. And it does not take much reflection or experience of life to see the truth of this. All the same, we still find the lure of sexual immorality tantalizing. We play with the idea of it, and find ourselves diving in once again, even though in our hearts we know that it is both wrong and ultimately harmful.

Why is this?

"Do not be deceived"

Sexual sins have a deceptive quality to them. They often deceive us into thinking that they represent the good life, rather than the judgement of God. Notice what God says about this in the letter to the Ephesians:

> But among you there must not be even a hint of sexual immorality, or of any kind of impurity, or of greed, because these are improper for God's holy people. Nor should there be obscenity, foolish talk or coarse joking, which are out of place, but rather thanksgiving. For of this you can be sure: No immoral, impure or greedy person–such a man is an idolater–has any inheritance in the kingdom of Christ and of God. Let no-one deceive you with empty words, for because of such things God's wrath comes on those who are disobedient. (Ephesians 5:3-6).

Here is a warning about the deceptive, but ultimately empty, words of those who downplay the seriousness of immorality. Those who practise these things have no inheritance in the kingdom. Much the same thing is said to the Corinthians:

> Do you not know that the wicked will not inherit the kingdom of God? Do not be deceived: Neither the sexually immoral nor idolaters nor adulterers nor male prostitutes nor those who practise homosexuality nor thieves nor the greedy nor drunkards nor slanderers nor swindlers will inherit the kingdom of God. (1 Corinthians 6:9-10).

Again, there is a warning not to be deceived by the seeming attractiveness of sin. But notice the make-up of the list of offences, both in Ephesians and in 1 Corinthians. Sexual immorality is part of the sinfulness that will exclude one from the kingdom of God, but it is not the only part. Greed and slander and drunkenness are just as bad. For social reasons, we may have a higher repugnance towards one sort of sin than another, but in God's eyes there is no distinction. Sin is sin, and if you are greedy or slanderous or drunken, then you have no place in the kingdom of God.

Sexual sin is deceptive in another way. It traps us in a net of denial and guilt, and reinforces our rebellion against God. Once we have sinned sexually, we become powerfully motivated to keep God at bay. We cling to our sin, and grow to love it; and we refuse to accept that it might be wrong, because 'it felt so right'. As Romans 1 put it, our thinking becomes futile, and our hearts are darkened. We say to Evil, "Be thou my good". God becomes a distant adversary, whose very existence we can hardly bring ourselves to acknowledge, for to do so would be to overthrow everything. This attitude is expressed in the Gospel of John in referring to people's rejection of Jesus:

> This is the verdict: Light has come into the world, but men loved darkness instead of light because their deeds were evil. Everyone who does evil hates the light, and will not come into the light for fear that his deeds will be exposed (John 3:19-20).

Sexual immorality is by no means the only sin that affects us in this way, but it is a powerful one. The cycle is self-reinforcing. We rebel against God, and reject his rule over our lives. We try to live our own way, under our own rules, but we find that nothing works out how we thought. God gives us over to the consequences of our rebellion, which include both the practice and the destructive effects of sexual immorality. And the immorality only serves to reinforce and strengthen our rejection of God, for the very mention of his name pricks our conscience, and hardens our resolve to reject him. To come anywhere near him would require an admission of guilt.

In this cycle, which is the sad story of humanity's history, we also see the tale of the last 100 years or so mapped out. Like Adam and Eve, and all humanity before them, Western society has rebelled against God. We have rejected his revelation, denied his goodness, abandoned his wisdom. And as a society, God has indeed given us over to the consequences of our folly. We have not only plunged into immorality, but have deceived ourselves (often with false research) into thinking that it really is perfectly all right.

We can no longer pretend that it is all right. The sexual revolution has been a failed rebellion. It is, in essence, the same failed rebellion as Adam and Eve's. We longed for freedom, for the absence of restraint, for the power to make our own rules. We discovered instead that we have unleashed a whirlwind of personal and social problems whose effects will be felt into the next millennium.

Sex in our society is off the rails. It is out of control. And this leads us to ask: Is there any way out of this mess?

CHAPTER 6

The way we were

Imagine a community in which sexual immorality is rife; in which adultery, prostitution, homosexuality, theft, drunkenness and disorder are common.

Welcome to the world of the New Testament. It was a world in which (at least sexually speaking) many modern people would have felt at home. It was a place in which, like the late twentieth century, sex was off the rails.

This was the world into which Christ came, and in which the movement that bears his name was born and flourished. Although the cultural trappings were different–in terms of language and dress and custom–it is a world we recognize as our own. The New Testament speaks to the human situation, in which people have conducted a revolution against God and have suffered the consequences. It speaks of the real world, in which people use and abuse each other, and in which relationships break down, in which people know lots about sex but not so much about love.

However, the New Testament also speaks of hope, of

the possibility of redemption and of change. In this chapter, we will look at what that hope is, and at how we can make it our own.

There are many ways we could begin, none better than by looking again at the Apostle Paul's first letter to Christians in the port city of Corinth:

> Do you not know that the wicked will not inherit the kingdom of God? Do not be deceived: Neither the sexually immoral nor idolaters nor adulterers nor male prostitutes nor homosexual offenders nor thieves nor the greedy nor drunkards nor slanderers nor swindlers will inherit the kingdom of God. And that is what some of you were (1 Corinthians 6:9-11a).

And that is what some of you were. The church at Corinth, to which these words were written, contained ex-adulterers, ex-prostitutes, ex-thieves, ex-drunkards, ex-homosexual offenders, ex-slanderers, ex-swindlers–pretty much ex-anything you care to name. Corinth was that kind of town. It had a reputation all over the ancient world for sexual promiscuity and degeneracy. And in their former lifestyle, some of those who were now Christians had done their share.

For them, however, it was in the past. What had happened to change them? The answer comes in the following sentence.

> But you were washed, you were sanctified, you were justified in the name of the Lord Jesus Christ and by the Spirit of our God (1 Corinthians 6:11b).

The very important little word 'but' is repeated three times in the original Greek language of the text: "*but* you were washed; *but* you were sanctified; *but* you were justified in the name of the Lord Jesus Christ and by the Spirit of our God".

We will think more about the details of what this sentence means shortly, but its basic thrust is clear, and this is the central truth of Christianity–*that God has done something about the mess we're in, and he has done it through Jesus Christ.* 'Judgement' is not God's final word for mankind. There is a 'but'. God does not leave humanity simply to suffer the consequences. He takes the initiative to do something.

What exactly has God done? What do the words of 1 Corinthians 6:11 mean?

A new start

The text says that the once notoriously sinful Corinthians were 'washed', 'sanctified' and 'justified'. These words (at least the latter two) may seem strange to us, but the ideas that they convey are quite straightforward. They all refer in different ways to the fact that through the work of Jesus, there has been a decisive break with the immorality of the past. Jesus came to bring not a new law code, or a new morality, but forgiveness and a new start.

This forgiveness is based on the central event of the Christian gospel, the crucifixion of Jesus. The message of the New Testament is that through dying on the cross, Jesus took upon himself the punishment that we deserve for our rebellion against God. He died in our place, as a substitute. In Jesus' own words, he died to pay the 'ransom' or debt that we owed (Mark 10:45). The substitutionary death of Jesus makes forgiveness possible. It allows us to be *washed clean* from all our sins; it allows us to be acquitted of our wrongdoing (which is what 'justified' means).

This is the message of the New Testament on page after page, which makes it all the more extraordinary that Christianity is so often portrayed as simply a religion of 'morality' or 'being good'. If biblical Christianity is about anything, it is about the fact that we are *not* good–none of us–that we have failed and rebelled against God, and that only through the initiative of God in Jesus Christ can we be reconciled to God.

Confusing Christianity with moral uprightness and respectability is not only a modern problem. It is one that Jesus himself faced with the religious authorities of his day. The following episode is a case in point:

> Now one of the Pharisees invited Jesus to have dinner with him, so he went to the Pharisee's house and reclined at the table. When a woman who had lived a sinful life in that town learned that Jesus was eating at the Pharisee's house, she brought an alabaster jar of perfume, and as she stood behind him at his feet weeping, she began to wet his feet with her tears. Then she wiped them with her hair, kissed them and poured perfume on them.
>
> When the Pharisee who had invited him saw this, he said to himself, "If this man were a prophet, he would know who is touching him and what kind of woman she is–that she is a sinner."
>
> Jesus answered him, "Simon, I have something to tell you."

> "Tell me, teacher," he said.
>
> "Two men owed money to a certain moneylender. One owed him five hundred denarii, and the other fifty. Neither of them had the money to pay him back, so he cancelled the debts of both. Now which of them will love him more?"
>
> Simon replied, "I suppose the one who had the bigger debt cancelled."
>
> "You have judged correctly," Jesus said. Then he turned towards the woman and said to Simon, "Do you see this woman? I came into your house. You did not give me any water for my feet, but she wet my feet with her tears and wiped them with her hair. You did not give me a kiss, but this woman, from the time I entered, has not stopped kissing my feet. You did not put oil on my head, but she has poured perfume on my feet. Therefore, I tell you, her many sins have been forgiven–for she loved much. But he who has been forgiven little loves little."
>
> Then Jesus said to her, "Your sins are forgiven."
>
> The other guests began to say among themselves, "Who is this who even forgives sins?" (Luke 7:36-49).

The expectations of the religiously respectable people are confounded by the way Jesus treats the woman. Her outpouring of love and gratitude to Jesus is a result of how much she has been forgiven. Her debt has been cancelled.

This is the very essence of Jesus' mission–to "seek and save the lost" (as Jesus puts it later in Luke's Gospel).

He was on a rescue mission, and his death was the means by which the rescue could ultimately take place. No-one was 'too sinful'. In fact, the more sinful you were, the more there was to be forgiven; and the more you were forgiven, the more copious would be the expressions of love and gratitude in return.

For the Corinthians, with all that they had been involved in, this was good news. No matter how much of a mess their lives were in, no matter what they had done to others, no matter how much they had rebelled against God and all that he stood for, no matter how 'dirty' they were as a result of their sin–they could now be washed clean. No matter how guilty they were before God, they could now be declared 'not guilty', because Jesus had stepped in and taken their punishment upon himself.

This is the breathtaking message of Christianity–not that we all have to try to be good to earn God's favour, but that *having failed dismally* to earn God's favour, we can be forgiven and washed clean and accepted back by him.

Amazingly, there is even more, and it comes out in the meaning of the (to us) unusual word 'sanctified'.

Holier than who?

The imagery of being 'sanctified' or 'made holy' (another way of saying the same thing) means something rather different to modern people than it did to recipients of 1 Corinthians. To many people, a 'sanctified' or 'holy' person is an aloof, pious, religious type, who carries an air of superiority, stuffiness and moral purity (at least on the outside).

However, in the first century, 'sanctified' was a more straightforward sort of word. It meant 'to be set apart for a particular purpose', 'to be special and distinctive'. In modern terms, we might say that a football referee is 'sanctified' for the purpose of adjudicating on the field. He has a completely different function and place within the game than the players, and for a particular purpose. He has his own rooms in the grandstand, his own uniform on the field. You can spot him straight away. His whole appearance, behaviour and role is quite distinctive. He is sanctified (or 'made holy') by the footballing authorities for the role of referee.

This is very much what Paul means by his words to the Corinthians. The Corinthians had been given a new start. They had been washed clean from the dirt of their previous behaviour; they had been 'justified' (or declared acquitted) from their wrong-doing; and they had also been 'sanctified'. That is, as part of this radical change in their circumstances, they had been set apart to be God's special people, to be different from those around them, to live a different sort of life.

To put it another way, God didn't send his Son to die on our behalf so that we could simply go back to living the same old destructive lifestyle. His overall purpose was to set apart a group of people who would be 'his people', who would live his way, who would be free from the damaging behaviour of their past and would lead new lives. In another of his letters, Paul expresses this idea very clearly:

> For the grace of God that brings salvation has appeared to all men. It teaches us to say "No" to ungodliness and worldly passions, and to live self-controlled, upright and godly lives in this present age, while we wait for the blessed hope–

> the glorious appearing of our great God and Saviour, Jesus Christ, who gave himself for us to redeem us from all wickedness and to purify for himself a people that are his very own, eager to do what is good (Titus 2:11-14).

Note how God's grace and salvation comes first, and as a result of it Christians are motivated to say 'No' to ungodliness and worldly passions, and to live good and upright lives while they wait for Jesus to return. Notice also what the overall plan is–that Jesus Christ gave himself for us (i.e. died on the cross for us) so that he might "purify for himself a people that are his very own, eager to do what is good". Ultimately, this purified people will share eternity with him.

This was God's purpose, the Bible tells us, from the very beginning. God had it in mind to save a people for himself who would stand apart from the rest of the world, and live life as it was meant to be lived, according to the ways of the Creator. God's ultimate answer to the disaster of Adam and Eve is to create a new people, called out from among the rest, who would live distinctively as his people, in accordance with the true order and nature of the world.

Coming back to the Corinthians, we can see why such a sharp contrast is drawn between what they once *were*, and what they now *are*:

> And that is what some of you were. But you were washed, you were sanctified, you were justified in the name of the Lord Jesus Christ and by the Spirit of our God (1 Corinthians 6:11).

They had been sanctified–that is, set apart to be different, to live as God created us to live.

God in us

One other thing needs to be said before we turn to think about how all this applies specifically to sex. It relates to a phrase that we've glossed over so far in our unpacking of 1 Corinthians 6–that God's plan takes place not only through the Lord Jesus Christ, but also by "the Spirit of our God".

The change that took place in the Corinthians was not simply something external to them. It was not only that their past mistakes had been forgiven, and that they had a new purpose and orientation in life–it was also that God himself had come to live within them by his Spirit.

God does not set us apart as his special people to live in holiness and just leave us to it. In his great kindness, he also works *within us* to change us, to drive and motivate us, to prompt and enable us to obey him, to give us the power we need to turn away from the past and begin to lead a new life.

Changing the wrong attitudes and behaviours that come so naturally to us is not easy. It takes time. It takes effort. In fact, it takes more than we, in our own power, can muster. The Bible makes very clear that the new life of the Christian is not a bed of roses. It is a struggle to get rid of the destructive habits of our former way of life, and to adopt God's way of living. That, after all, is the point of the passage we have been reading in 1 Corinthians 6–it urges us not to return to our former manner of life, but to live consistently with our new status.

God does not leave his newly washed, acquitted

and set apart people to fight this battle alone. He aids and strengthens them by his own presence within. He comes to dwell in them by his Spirit.

God's way and the world's

The liberating message that biblical Christianity holds out for a society such as ours is made all the more stark by the obvious failure of the alternatives. The world, in its rejection of God, can only face the kinds of problems thrown up by the sexual revolution by reverting to such chestnuts as "We need more education". Yet this too has been a manifest failure.

Although sex education is doubtless of some value, it is naive to think that merely making teenagers better informed about sexual choices will somehow result in more responsible behaviour. In fact, there is strong evidence that comprehensive sex education has made little difference in places where it has been tried.[1] This failure is no surprise, because the problem is not one of information (or lack thereof) but of heart. Sex education cannot deal with the guilt and consequences of past mistakes, nor can it motivate a change in behaviour or a desire to make restitution for wrongs that have been done.

The modern secular world's solutions to the tangled mess of modern sexuality are ultimately all utilitarian–

---

1. Again writing in *The Atlantic Monthly* (Oct, 1994), Barbara Defoe Whitehead mounts a compelling argument that the programme of 'comprehensive sex education' that has been conducted in many states in America has done nothing to achieve its stated aims–that is, to reduce the incidence of teenage pregnancy and sexually transmitted diseases.

that is, they are based on trying to work out which course of action will produce the most human happiness. (As we have already seen, this was essentially Bertrand Russell's sexual ethic.) However, utilitarianism is itself so fraught with problems as to be almost useless for this task. It is essentially a 'wait and see' philosophy, which embarks on a course of action in the expectation that it will lead to a happy outcome, but with no real way of knowing whether the outcome will be happy until we get there. Putting to one side the insoluble questions of how one measures or even defines 'happiness', the obvious question is: how long do we wait? Is 35 years long enough (in the case of the sexual revolution)? Do we now declare the experiment a manifest failure? The evidence is certainly quite sufficient–the consequences of the sexual revolution have been almost uniformly disastrous–and yet many are still reluctant to admit it.

Those who are beginning to admit it are not always popular among their baby-boomer peers. In commenting on a recent conflict between Bettina Arndt (who is disturbed at the effects of the sexual revolution) and media commentator Richard Ackland (who refers to Arndt as 'Miss Prim'), Robert Manne makes a shrewd observation:

> Both Arndt and Ackland belong to the generation which fought for, observed the triumph of and experienced the benefits of the 60s cultural revolution of modernity. Concerning this revolution, this generation–my generation–is now beginning to divide.
>
> One part still looks upon the progressive emancipation of the individual from the ties of

> family and community obligation, and from all restraints on the gratification of individual desire, as an unambiguous good. Their instinct is to close their eyes to the mounting evidence of consequent social disintegration and harm. Another part, however, is beginning to feel anxious about certain unexpected or unintended consequences of the revolution in which they once invested their energies and hopes.[2]

For those who are anxious about where we have come to–like Arndt, Helen Garner, Richard Neville, Robert Manne, and others–the question remains: what do we do about it? Utilitarianism can only suggest a solution that might (or might not) produce happiness for some people some time in the future, with no guarantees and no way of knowing till we get there.

The image that springs to mind is of a mass of people walking in darkness, stumbling towards a hoped-for freedom, but having no idea from whence they have come, where they are going or what abyss might lie in their path.

The message of biblical Christianity is that God is light, and that in the person of his Son, Jesus Christ, that light has come into the world. In the face of the hard realities of sexual immorality, impurity, debauchery and all the rest, God shines a light to break the darkness. In the words of 1 Corinthians, he says 'but'! He brings the possibility of forgiveness and a new start through the death of Jesus; he sets his people apart for a new lifestyle

---

2. Robert Manne, "The modern reality of social revolution" in *The Sydney Morning Herald,* 25-5-98, p. 17.

that departs radically from the destructive behaviour of the past; and there he lives within us by his Spirit, to lead and enable us to put that lifestyle into operation.

This message of hope applies as much to sex as it does to any other aspect of our lives. What it means specifically for sex is the subject of our next chapter. However, a prior and more basic question must first be confronted by each of us personally: Have we turned back to God to be washed, sanctified and justified, or not?

If we have not, then we need to resolve this question before much progress can be made. Further thinking and investigation may be necessary, and some additional information can be found in Appendix 3. However, there really are only two alternatives. The argument of this book (and the Bible) is that the terrible mess humanity is in with regard to sex (and everything else) is a direct consequence of our basic rebellion against the Creator, and our rejection of his ways. We can return to him, and grasp the lifeline of hope that he has held out to us in Christ. Or we can continue in rebellion, with all its destructive consequences.

For some readers, the decision to turn back to God is one that they have taken already. If this is so, then, as the next chapter will outline, our behaviour and attitude to sex is simply one more area of life in which we must stand apart as one of God's special people, turning our backs on the distorted patterns that the rest of the world follows, and living God's way, as we were created to.

CHAPTER 7

Pure Sex

At last, you may think dear reader, we are getting to the important part–to the practical details of dealing with our sexuality.

However, the important part of this book has already been reached. This chapter is more of a tying up of the loose ends. The pinnacle of our argument is Christ, who brings God's plans to fruition, and reconciles our tragically misguided and rebellious world to its Creator. As we have already seen, through Christ there is the possibility (and reality) of change–we can be forgiven our past mistakes ('washed') and declared free of guilt ('justified), and set apart as God's special people to do what is right and good in his eyes ('sanctified').

With all this in place, only the minor detail remains to be filled in, and much of it requires little elaboration. This is, in fact, one of the distinctive features of biblical Christianity (although historically Christians have not always grasped this). It is not a legalistic religion, with reams of regulations and ordinances and detailed codes of behaviour. It is primarily about what Jesus Christ has done, and how we gladly respond to that in every facet of our lives. It's about a radical change in our status before God (from condemned to forgiven) which results in a new lifestyle of joyful obedience.

In other words, if we have embraced the essential truth of the Christian gospel for ourselves, and are thus driven by love and gratitude and the Spirit of God to live as one of God's holy people in all that we do, then we have learnt most of what we need to know about sex.

Let us clarify this, before touching on some practical detail.

Pure sex is pure sex

The basic message of this book has been that pure sex is good sex. Sex that God regards as holy, right and pure is sex as it was meant to be, as it was created to be– unadulterated, free, 100% proof, genuine and joyous. Pure sex.

There is only one place to find pure sex, according to God, and that is within the utterly committed relationship we call 'marriage'. Only in marriage can sex do successfully what it is meant to do. Only in this sort of sex is the 'nudity' we seek ultimately possible. This is not to say, of course, that all sex that takes place within all marriages everywhere will be equally wonderful, but we will say more about this below.

The biblical path to pure sex may be a road less travelled in these times, but it is no less attractive for being so. In fact, one thing that drives us towards God's way is that it actually accords with reality. God created the world. He knows how it goes. He knows what works. God's purposes for sex, and therefore his framework for sex, aren't an arbitrary list of life-denying rules set up to test us, or to discipline us. They spring from the way things are, the way the world is ordered and made, the way *we* are ordered and made.

To commit oneself to God's way, then, may be to depart from the majority, but it is not to depart from normality. On the contrary, it is to depart from abnormality. It is to turn back from a distorted, deceptive unreality which only damages us and other people.

This is what holiness or being 'sanctified' really means (as we began to see in chapter 6). God's people are set apart, or special. They are distinctive, not in that they live a weird, artificial existence, but because they now live rightly, wisely, purely. They stand out like beacons in a dark world. They have turned back from unreality to reality, and so they are distinctive, separate, and to the rest of the world 'strange'.

As we also saw in our last chapter, this is the very reason God has saved us and forgiven us through the death of his Son. This is the purpose of the plan. And this is why Christians will strive for holiness and purity in all that they do, including sex. As the Bible puts it:

> For this is God's will: your sanctification. This means keeping clear of all sexual immorality, and for each person to take a wife for himself in holiness and honour, not in passionate lust like the heathen, who do not know God (1 Thessalonians 4:3-5 our translation).

For the Christian, who *does* know God, holiness will be an absolute priority, for we know this is the very reason God has saved us–for holiness. Whatever thoughts or decisions or actions we take with regard to sex and marriage, holiness will be foremost in our minds.

This means that as we relate to each other, we will do so with absolute purity, as Paul commands Timothy:

> Treat older women as mothers, and younger women as sisters, with absolute purity (1 Timothy 5:2).

We will avoid sexual immorality, and not be deceived by it. We will swim against the tide of our society's obsession with sex, and be thought crazy for doing so, as Peter suggests:

> For you have spent enough time in the past doing what pagans choose to do–living in debauchery, lust, drunkenness, orgies, carousing and detestable idolatry. They think it strange that you do not plunge with them into the same flood of dissipation, and they heap abuse on you. But they will have to give account to him who is ready to judge the living and the dead (1 Peter 4:3-5).

As a result of our absolute commitment to holiness, we will make decisions that the rest of the world–including our families and friends–find it impossible to understand.

Perhaps the best way to tease out what this means in practice is under the headings of singleness and marriage.

Sex and the single

Singleness occupies a strange place in our culture. At one level, it is the land of the free; the life without burdensome responsibility and domestic restrictions. Yet at the same time, it is the life that most people seem keen to leave behind. Somehow, we sense that God was right in the garden of Eden when he observed "It is not good for the man to be alone".

In fact, it is to relieve loneliness–deep, personal loneliness–that many single people seek refuge in sex. In sex, there is intimacy, relationship and emotional nudity. Sex creates a bond with someone. It forges some kind of relationship. Used outside God's framework, however, it is also damaging. It bonds us to someone who may pull away (sometimes only too quickly), leaving us scarred and even more alone than before.

Christians will be counter-cultural at this point. They will say, "You don't understand. Sex is great, but it was designed by God to do certain things, to achieve certain things, and these things are only achieved in marriage. If you misuse sex, you'll only do damage somehow or other." Knowing that God's purposes for sex lie within marriage, unmarried Christians will regard sex as simply outside their experience, as belonging to a stage in life they have not yet entered, or may never enter.

Even if a relationship has begun, and there is some possibility it might move towards marriage, sex still belongs among the joys we anticipate for the future, not that we dabble in at present. Until there is real commitment to one another–that is, until there is marriage–we should treat each other, as Paul says, with absolute purity, like brothers and sisters.

There is little point trying to lay down detailed regulations about all this, and to legislate precisely what is permissible or not. The principle is quite clear, as is the rationale for it: You're not married, so don't do it. Nor is it possible to draw an arbitrary line somewhere between kissing and intercourse and say "That's where the sex begins–you can go that far and no further!" Sex is sex, and most couples have no difficulty in determining when they are being 'sexual' with each other. Out of love for the other person, and a desire to please God, and a knowledge of the truth about sex, we will abstain.[1]

There is, of course, more to say about the struggles of living this out in our promiscuous world, and indeed about the peculiar possibilities opened up for singleness by Christianity, but first let us turn to sex and marriage.

The slavery of marriage

That marriage is slavery is quite true. It is an unconditional, lifelong commitment to another person; a commitment to place oneself at the other's disposal, to love them, serve them, and care for them, no matter

---

1. Some readers may be wondering where masturbation fits into this scenario. Given what we have seen of God's purposes for sex, masturbation cannot be regarded as a satisfactory alternative. It has nothing to do with either companionship or producing children! All the same, the Bible does not condemn the practice–in fact, it doesn't even mention it. It is probably best to regard masturbation as a fairly neutral 'coping mechanism' that some individuals may find useful at different times to relieve sexual pressure or frustration. Given the Bible's silence on the subject, it would seem unnecessary to treat masturbation as a 'taboo', or as a matter for guilt.

what circumstances may arise. Mutual slavery, but slavery no less.

However, in that 'slavery' we find all that makes marriage beautiful, desirable and ultimately successful. It is one of those paradoxes of life that in loving someone else we find all the joy we hoped to find in being loved ourselves. Just as God is love, and his Son, Christ Jesus, embodied love, so we find that written into the very fabric of the creation is the beauty, worthiness and rightness of love. And by 'love', we don't mean romance or infatuation or even an emotion. We mean the settled intention, expressed in a myriad of actions, to seek the good of another.

This was Christ's basic command, that we follow his example of self-sacrificial love, of giving his very life for the sake of others. The New Testament applies this specifically to marriage:

> Husbands, love your wives, just as Christ loved the church and gave himself up for her to make her holy, cleansing her by the washing with water through the word, and to present her to himself as a radiant church, without stain or wrinkle or any other blemish, but holy and blameless. In this same way, husbands ought to love their wives as their own bodies. He who loves his wife loves himself. After all, no-one ever hated his own body, but he feeds and cares for it, just as Christ does the church–for we are members of his body (Ephesians 5:25-30).

The modern idea of fostering 'independence' in marriage–as if this somehow strengthened the marriage bond–quite misunderstands what marriage is and how it works. Marriage is not about maintaining my integrity as an individual, creating my own space, and existing in a negotiated peace with another individual seeking to do the same.

On the contrary, marriage in God's purposes is about uniting myself to someone of the opposite sex such that his or her welfare becomes my welfare; his or her sorrow my sorrow; his or her pleasure my pleasure.

Thus sex in marriage is also a matter of slavery, as we have seen before:

> The husband should fulfil his marital duty to his wife, and likewise the wife to her husband. The wife's body does not belong to her alone but also to her husband. In the same way, the husband's body does not belong to him alone but also to his wife (1 Corinthians 7:3-4).

Really good sex in a marriage depends on a variety of factors, but by far the most important is the commitment of each partner to *serve the other's sexual needs*, rather than their own. It is first of all about the quality of the relationship, and the motivation of a changed heart to serve the other person, rather than any particular sexual technique.

If we can speak for a moment in very broad generalizations, and from the light of accumulated wisdom, most husbands need to learn to take time over sex–both before and during. For men, sexual arousal and satisfaction can happen very quickly, and be quite unaffected by their mood or what's been happening previously. He can come home from work, tired and stressed, growl at the kids, sullenly watch TV for a couple of hours, and then catch sight of his wife in her night-dress as she slides into bed next to him and be raring to go.

For most women, this is almost incomprehensible. Her sexual response is usually slower, and more conditioned by how she's feeling (especially how she's feeling towards her husband), by her mood, the atmosphere, how much time she has spent with her partner that evening, whether she's had a bad day, or what time of the month it is. A wise husband, who wants to love his wife and meet her sexual needs, learns that sex starts long before bed. The more comfortable, relaxed and 'loved' a wife feels, the more satisfying the sex is likely to be for her, and ultimately for him as well. Once the sex begins, the loving husband takes time; he will wait for his wife, and focus on giving her pleasure, rather than on simply satisfying his own desires.

Again speaking very generally, for wives, serving a husband's sexual needs may mean being willing to muster some enthusiasm for sex when not being particularly in the mood. Most men feel like sex more often than most women (although this is not always the case), and the loving wife will make allowances for this–just as the loving husband will also not be insistent or demanding or selfish in demanding sex on tap. Paradoxically, many women find that in serving their husbands, and focusing on his pleasure, their own response is awakened and increased.

To be candid, living this way can be a battle. It is a constant struggle against our most basic instinct, which is to be selfish. Yet it is ultimately what makes marriages work. It is not poor communication that causes marriages to fail, or incompatibility, or financial problems, or the pressure of children. These things may be the symptoms, but the ultimate cause is lack of love–or to put it another way, selfishness and sin. And because we are all sinners, no marriage is immune from conflict, argument, emotional pain and loneliness. Sex can be part of the problem; or part of the solution. It can be a cause of conflict, bitterness and regret. Or it can function as God intended–as a strong adhesive to bind two people together in a lifelong union, in spite of their differences and their conflict.

The future of intimacy

Marriage is a good part of God's creation. It allows and fosters an intimacy between two people that is one of life's great joys. Yet, this intimacy and fellowship only works because it is exclusive and permanent. It cannot be shared around. Because of the nature of this created world, that level of intimacy and relationship is only appropriate between two people, a man and a woman.

In the next world, however, things will be different, as Jesus explained to the sceptical Sadducees:

> At the resurrection people will neither marry nor be given in marriage; they will be like the angels in heaven (Matthew 22:30).

Marriage, along with all of creation, is destined for transformation. In the resurrection, at the end of time, we will be part of a community of love and faithfulness and intimate fellowship that goes beyond the limits of earthly marriage. We will be in heaven.

This future-orientation helps us to keep earthly

marriage and singleness in perspective. Marriage is a good thing, to be enjoyed and valued. Yet it is not eternal. It will pass away, or be transformed, in eternity.

With singleness, the reverse is true. The single life can be very difficult, and in many ways seems to 'grate' against the created structures of God's world. The one thing that was 'not good' in Eden was the man's loneliness, and so God created woman so that humanity could live in married fellowship. Many single people can testify to how true all this is.

However, in the next age 'singleness' too will be transformed. We will all live in intimate fellowship. None of us will be alone. And in the kindness of God, we can have a taste of this heavenly fellowship now–in the Christian congregation. The love, fellowship, mutual commitment and faithfulness that we seek to live out in our churches, is a mirror or foretaste of our heavenly fellowship. And this fellowship provides an environment in which singleness is actually a possibility as a viable lifestyle. In the loving community of Christian fellowship, there is the potential for the single person to cope with the pressures of aloneness.

This is why the New Testament sees both marriage and singleness as worthy patterns of life. One affirms the goodness of God's creation. The other looks forward to the transformation of that creation. Both are good and right, in light of the coming age. Indeed, in view of our future hope, singleness has certain advantages. It is not only a possible option, but even an attractive one for the Christian, as we see in 1 Corinthians 7.

In this important passage about sex and marriage, the basic principle is that, given the circumstances,

Christians should basically *stay where they are*: "Each one should retain the place in life that the Lord assigned to him and to which God has called him. This is the rule I lay down in all the churches" (1 Corinthians 7:17). If married, they should remain so, and fulfil all the duties and enjoy all the pleasures (hence the passage quoted earlier about husbands and wives serving each other sexually). However, the passage goes on to say that if single, there is good reason to remain that way, unless circumstances dictate otherwise.

> Now to the unmarried and the widows I say: It is good for them to remain as I am. But if they can't control themselves, let them marry, for it is better to marry than to be aflame…
>
> Now about the young men and women: I have no command from the Lord, but I give a judgement as one who by the Lord's mercy is trustworthy. Because of the present crisis, I think that it is good for you to remain as you are. Are you married? Do not seek a divorce. Are you unmarried? Do not look for a wife. But if you do marry, you have not sinned; and if a young woman marries, she has not sinned. But those who marry will face many troubles in this life, and I want to spare you this.
>
> What I mean, brothers, is that the time is short. From now on those who have wives should live as if they had none; those who mourn, as if they did not; those who are rejoicing, as if they were not; those who buy something, as if it were not theirs to keep; those who use the things of the world, as if not engrossed in

> them. For this world in its present form is passing away.
>
> I would like you to be free from concern. An unmarried man is concerned about the Lord's affairs–how he can please the Lord. But a married man is concerned about the affairs of this world–how he can please his wife-–and his interests are divided. An unmarried woman or virgin is concerned about the Lord's affairs: Her aim is to be devoted to the Lord in both body and spirit. But a married woman is concerned about the affairs of this world–how she can please her husband. I am saying this for your own good, not to restrict you, but that you may live in a right way in undivided devotion to the Lord.
>
> If anyone thinks he is acting improperly towards the young woman he is engaged to, and if things are going too far, and he feels he ought to marry her, he should do as he wants. He is not sinning. They should get married. But the man who has settled the matter in his own mind, who is under no compulsion but has control over his own will, and who has made up his mind not to marry the young woman–this man also does the right thing. So then, he who marries the young woman does right, but he who does not marry her does even better. (1 Corinthians 7: 8-9, 25-38 our translation)

God's gift to each of us is the place he assigned to us in life. And we should be happy to stay put, and make the best of it, unless circumstances dictate a change. What are these circumstances? In the case of the married person, the only change possible is when your partner dies, or when your non-Christian partner deserts you. For the unmarried, the circumstances for change have to do with lacking self-control, being "aflame" and "acting improperly" (vv. 9, 36). In these circumstances, it is much better to marry. If this seems to us a little clinical, or not quite a worthy motive for marriage, perhaps it is because we have too romantic a view of marriage, and not romantic enough a view of sex.

All the same, there is little doubt that Paul sees singleness not only as an option in the Christian community, but in light of our hope in the coming of Christ, and the urgency of doing his work, a very positive option. In fact, all things being equal, Paul advises his readers to remain single unless there is a good reason to marry. We live in 'the last days', and the single person is free to do much for the work of the Lord. Although marriage is a good part of creation, it is part of the world that is passing away.

This is such an explosive suggestion in our modern context that many readers will find it a 'hard saying'. The idea that singleness might be a good and worthwhile state for the Christian, and marriage an option to pursue if our circumstances dictate–this is almost more than we can cope with. Most of us have been raised with the expectation of marriage and family, and we may never have even considered the possibility of pursuing singleness as a positive alternative. In our Christian culture, the single person is regarded as someone to be pitied. He or she is something of a reject.

However, this only indicates how much modern Christianity has absorbed the values and culture of our own society, rather than God's. If we are to do more than play at being Christian, we must take God at his word, and trust him. Singleness is not bad. Far from it—it may well be the good place God has assigned us, as we wait and work within the fellowship of his people.

Just as the person who relentlessly pursues happiness for its own sake often finds it frustratingly elusive, so the single person who thinks of nothing but marriage may not only find it elusive, but life rather miserable in the meantime. Many single people find that having given up their fixation with marriage, and attacked life with a positive attitude, there is much to be gained—in contentment, in satisfaction, and in worthwhile work for God that can be done.

And if it is within God's purposes for us to find a partner, we can be confident that it will happen in his good time.[2]

---

2. For a treatment of the often confusing subject of God's guidance, and how it relates to singleness and marriage, see our earlier publication *Guidance and the voice of God*. (Matthias Media, 1996). More details on page 136.

Epilogue

In his idiosyncratically brilliant work, *Orthodoxy*, G. K. Chesterton compares his 'discovery' of the truth of orthodox Christianity to a yachtsman who, through a navigational error, ends up landing on the shore of his native England, while thinking that he has discovered an exotic South Sea island. Though he may look like a fool, says Chesterton, the yachtsman does not feel like one. On the contrary, he realises that his mistake was a most enviable one, because he has enjoyed all the fascinating terrors of discovery along with all the humane security of coming home again.

It seems to us that our society is also like this lost yachtsman, but with a difference–we are far from our home shore. We have embarked on a journey which we thought was to a better world, a world of liberation, sexual adventure and expanding our horizons. Yet, as a culture, we find ourselves lost, dismasted, and taking a lot of water. Having rejected God, we found that the morality we clung to in his absence had no power. Having rejected that morality, we have created a nightmare from which we cannot seem to awake. We wanted freedom and sexual intimacy, but we found instead a different sort of slavery, and destructive consequences we didn't expect.

In many ways, the message of this book has been quite simply, "Go back!". And it is our hope that for some readers, this call will have made sense. Like the yachtsman landing unknowingly on his home soil, it may have seemed at first new, radical, even terrifying. And yet at the same time, strangely familiar, and reassuringly like home. For while the view of sex we have been proposing is indeed radical as far as twentieth century society is concerned, it is by no means new. It is drawn from the ancient texts of Christianity. It represents the wisdom of the Creator of the world, who made us, and sex, in his own good way and for his own good purposes.

This is home. It is where sex makes sense, and works. It is where we were always meant to be. Indeed, to extend the metaphor further, this is why God sent his Son, Jesus Christ, into the world–to go out and find us, and bring us home; to offer forgiveness and a new start; to provide us with the power to change.

For those readers who are already Christians, it is not of course about coming home, but about realizing afresh that we have been brought home, and that home is the place to be. We must not envy the world its sexual 'freedom', for the world is not free–it is lost.

And there but for God's grace go we.

APPENDIX 1

Homosexuality and pure sex

The high public profile of homosexuality has been one of the most striking features of the sexual landscape in the final quarter of the twentieth century. As psychoanalyst and social critic Charles Socarides has put it: "from the love that dare not speak its name to the love that can't shut up–in barely 25 years".

Over the past generation, the public profile of homosexuality has changed enormously. In the 1960s, a public figure who openly declared that he was gay, or spoke favourably of homosexuality in some way, would have been treated at the very least with suspicion, and more probably as an outcast. Now, the reverse is true. Anything less than a positive endorsement of the homosexual lifestyle renders one liable to the charge of 'homophobia', which ranks along with sexism and racism as one of the deadly sins of modern society.

Positive images and stories about gays and their lifestyle are now part of our popular culture. Here in our home city, the Sydney Gay and Lesbian Mardi Gras is promoted as the most significant cultural and community event in the city's calendar, and is lauded by politicians as a symbol of civic maturity (not to mention a handy boost to the local economy). Gay themes are now commonplace in TV, film, art, and literature. Gay is now firmly part of the mainstream. Almost without our realizing it, Western society has moved from deep suspicion and condemnation of homosexuality, through tolerance, to open acceptance and promotion of its benefits–or at least, that is the perception commonly portrayed by our opinion leaders and shapers.

How has this happened? And is it a good thing? How does it relate to 'pure sex'?

In this appendix, we will consider homosexuality, and how it relates to the argument we have been developing in this book. As we do so, we will first consider homosexuality in general, as a phenomenon and as a public movement, before turning to how it affects us as individuals.

The place to start, as always, is with God and his purposes.

God's purposes for sex

As we saw in chapter 6, the Bible is no stranger to homosexuality. And its message to homosexuals is much the same as its message to those who practise other forms of sexual immorality. It is a message not simply of criticism or judgement, but of forgiveness and hope.

It would be wrong, however, to pretend that the criticism wasn't there. In relation to God's created purposes for sex–that is, the production of children and the formation of a deep personal union between a man and woman–homosexuality represents just one of the ways in which humanity rebels against God. Homosexual sex is a disordered form of sex. It cuts across and frustrates the structures and purposes of God's creation. In this sense, it is similar to adultery, fornication (that is sex before marriage), bestiality, rape, prostitution or incest. These are all wrong expressions of sexuality–not in some arbitrary way (as we have argued above), but because they are fundamentally at odds with the good purposes for which God created sexuality.

Thus, homosexual sex (both gay and lesbian) is condemned in the Scriptures. In recent times, some have attempted to find ways around these biblical prohibitions, but the arguments are weak, and others have adequately refuted them.[1] The Bible is quite clear in its attitude, and in a sense we would expect it to be. Given the basic foundations of biblical sexuality in Genesis, it would be extraordinary if homosexuality was regarded as anything else but a distortion of God's good created order.

As with the Bible's view on sexuality as a whole, this attitude towards homosexuality, while ringing true for some people, is felt by a great many others to be off the planet. After all, isn't being gay an entirely normal and relatively common thing? And aren't people born gay anyway? Isn't it a perfectly valid lifestyle?

---

1. For helpful analyses of these arguments, see T. Schmidt, *Straight and Narrow? Compassion and Clarity in the Homosexual Debate*, (Leicester: IVP, 1995), ch 2-5, and A. Shead, "Homosexuality and the church: historical survey" in B. G. Webb (ed) *Theological and Pastoral Responses to Homosexuality (Explorations 8)*, (Adelaide: Openbook, 1994), pp. 21-27.

The gay revolution

In chapters 3 and 4, we outlined a brief history of sex in our century. We looked at how much attitudes and behaviour had changed, and at some of the reasons for that change. It would be interesting to tell the same kind of story regarding homosexuality. A whole book would be required to do this. For our purposes, a few highlights will have to suffice.

The rise of homosexuality over the past 30 years or so has not simply been the result of a spontaneous recognition of how good homosexuality is; nor have a large percentage of the population 'come out' and declared their homosexuality. The homosexual community remains a very small minority. Depending on which survey you look to, the figure for males who are consistently homosexual is around 1% of the population. The figure for women is considerably less.

The gay and lesbian community are a small minority, but a very vocal and articulate one. Others have catalogued how successful the gay lobby has been in conducting a political campaign of protest and activism to 'normalize' homosexuality as a legitimate lifestyle.[2] In this campaign, the truth has often been a casualty. For example, homosexual activists now admit that the populist 10% figure drawn from Kinsey was a convenient exaggeration:

> The thing about the 'one in ten'–I think people probably always did know that it was inflated.

---

2. In particular, see Jeffrey Satinover's book, *Homosexuality and the Politics of Truth*, (Grand Rapids: Baker, 1996). Also see Shead *ibid*, pp 4-8 for a useful timeline.

> But it was a nice number that you could point to, that you say 'one in ten', and it's a really good way to get people to visualize that we're here.[3]

Truth is not the only casualty. The capacity for sound moral reasoning also seems to have been lost. For even if the figure were 10% or 20% or even 50%, of what relevance is this in discussing the rightness or wrongness of a course of action? If the majority of Australians approve of capital punishment (which repeated surveys show that they do), does that make capital punishment right? It makes it neither right nor wrong. Moral judgements cannot be made by statistics, although the gay lobby often seems to suggest otherwise. In their case, it is now quite apparent that even the statistics themselves were grossly exaggerated.

A similar level of exaggeration and misreporting occurred in relation to the alleged discovery of 'the gay gene' in 1993, and other biological studies that suggested that gays were 'born that way'. The studies concerned have been severely criticised, both for their methodology and conclusions, and in fact fall a long way short of demonstrating any definitive genetic or biological 'cause' for homosexuality.[4] Nevertheless, certain elements of the media were most willing to trumpet the finding that

---

3. A lesbian activist member of ACT-UP, quoted in J. Dallas, "Responding to Pro-Gay Theology" in G. R. Rekers (ed), *The Journal of Human Sexuality* (Carollton: Lewis and Stanley, 1996), p. 79.
4. See J. Satinover, pp. 109-117. Schmidt (pp. 131-159) also provides an analysis of the supposed discoveries, as well as a discussion of the wider issues of nature versus nurture in regard to sexuality.

'homosexuality was genetic', with the resulting influence on public opinion, and public policy.

Another key moment in the changing public attitudes to homosexuality took place some 20 years before. In 1973, the American Psychiatric Association (APA) voted to remove homosexuality from its list of psychiatric illnesses, and to classify it merely as a 'condition', like left-handedness. It has subsequently become clear that this decision was made not because of any new scientific evidence, or as part of a disinterested search for truth, but through a systematic campaign of political action on the part of gay activists. Indeed, at a crucial point in the debate, a letter was mailed by influential psychiatrists within the association to over 30,000 members of the APA, urging them to support the change. It was not revealed at the time that the letter was drafted and entirely funded by the National Gay Task Force.[5]

There is much more that could be said along these lines. It would be fruitful to examine, for example, how the gay agenda has become prominent in university faculties,[6] the role of TV, film and the print media in promoting homosexuality, and at how the rising tide of acceptance for homosexuality has also influenced

---

5. Satinover provides all the details (pp. 31-40), as well as further examples. He also has a helpful discussion of the complexities of defining homosexuality as an 'illness' when it might be more accurately described as a damaging behaviour pattern. Also see. C. Socarides, "How America Went Gay" in *The Journal of Human Sexuality*, pp. 29-32.

6. See Jerry Muller's fascinating account of this in "Coming Out Ahead: the Homosexual Moment in the Academy" in *First Things* 35 (Aug/Sept 1993), pp. 17-24.

Christian opinion, particularly among church hierarchies.

There is no doubt that the gay revolution has largely been a success, at least for homosexuals. Our opinion leaders and social gatekeepers have been won over to the cause, and will doubtless continue to promote the gay agenda, or at least benignly acquiesce in its advance. At another level, of course, it has been a social catastrophe.

The judgement of God

When AIDS first captured the public imagination in the late 1980s, it was widely discussed as to whether it constituted the 'judgement of God' upon homosexuality and the gay sub-culture. Was this new and terrible affliction God's way of indicating his disapproval?

We will not go into the details of this debate, except to note that the Bible approaches the question rather differently. As we have already seen in regard to sexual immorality generally, it is the *activity itself* which indicates God's judgement, not simply its harmful consequences. This is the point of Romans 1:18f. Because of our rejection of God, and our suppression of the truth, God in his righteous anger gives us over to the consequences of our rebellion, to a degraded and diminished existence.

> Therefore God gave them over in the sinful desires of their hearts to sexual impurity for the degrading of their bodies with one another. They exchanged the truth of God for a lie, and worshipped and served created things rather than the Creator – who is for ever praised. Amen. Because of this, God gave them over to shameful lusts. Even their women exchanged natural relations for unnatural ones. In the same way the men

> also abandoned natural relations with women and were inflamed with lust for one another. Men committed indecent acts with other men, and received in themselves the due penalty for their perversion. (Romans 1:24-27).

It is the practice of homosexuality itself–as with all sexual immorality–that fundamentally represents God's judgement on the world. Our rejection of God and his ways, and the order of his creation, leads to behaviours that scream out against who we are as God's creatures. To live this way is to live on the basis of the lie that God is not God, the wise creator of all. To then protest (too much) that it is a great lifestyle is more perverse still.

Sadly, it is becoming increasingly clear just how destructive a lifestyle it is. It is ironic that the surge of interest in all things homosexual over the past 15 years has led to a growing body of research that has, perhaps without intending to, demonstrated the true cost of the homosexual lifestyle. It is worth quoting at length from Jeffrey Satinover's summary of these findings:

> What would you think if a relative, friend, or colleague had a condition that is routinely, even if not always, associated with the following problems:
>
> - A significantly decreased likelihood of establishing or preserving a successful marriage
> - A five- to ten-year decrease in life expectancy
> - Chronic, potentially fatal, liver disease–hepatitis
> - Inevitably fatal esophageal cancer
> - Pneumonia
> - Internal bleeding

- Serious mental disabilities, many of which are irreversible
- A much higher than usual incidence of suicide
- A very low likelihood that its adverse effects can be eliminated unless the condition itself is eliminated
- An only 30 percent likelihood of being eliminated through lengthy, often costly, and very time-consuming treatment in an otherwise unselected population of sufferers (although a very high success rate among highly motivated, carefully selected sufferers)

...No doubt you would care deeply for someone close to you who had such a condition. And whether or not society considered it undesirable or even an illness, you would want to help. Undoubtedly, you would also consider it worth 'treating', that is, you would seek to help your relative, friend, or colleague by eliminating the condition entirely.

The condition we are speaking of is alcoholism. Alcoholism is clearly undesirable precisely because of all the adverse conditions directly associated with it, although not every alcoholic develops all the problems associated with it.

Alcoholism is a form of compulsive or addictive behaviour that has volitional, family, psychological, social, and genetic 'causes'. Whether it can be considered an 'illness' in the strict sense makes for an interesting philosophical discussion but a useless practical one–as is true for all addictions. Nonetheless, and in spite of the relatively modest 'cure' rate, it is still well worth treating, and treating as though it *were* an illness (as does organized psychiatry, which lists it as a disorder), because of the enormously serious personal and social consequences of not doing so.

Putting Two and Two Together

And now imagine another friend or colleague who had a condition associated with a similar list of problems:

- A significantly decreased likelihood of establishing or preserving a successful marriage
- A *twenty-five to thirty-year* decrease in life expectancy
- Chronic, potentially fatal, liver disease–infectious hepatitis, which increases the risk of liver cancer
- Inevitably fatal immune disease including associated cancers
- Frequently fatal rectal cancer
- Multiple bowel and other infectious diseases
- A much higher than usual incidence of suicide
- A very low likelihood that its adverse effects can be eliminated unless the condition itself is
- An at least 50 percent likelihood of being eliminated through lengthy, often costly, and very time-consuming treatment in an otherwise unselected group of sufferers (although a very high success rate, in some instances nearing 100 percent, for groups of highly motivated, carefully selected individuals)

...This condition is homosexuality. Yet despite the parallels between the two conditions, what is striking today are the sharply different responses to them.[7]

Despite all the spin doctoring, this is the reality of homosexuality, particularly among males. There is very little that is 'gay' about it. It is an appalling picture of humanity reaping the consequences of rebelling against God's good order.[8]

A gay response to this may be: "The path we take is risky; we know that. But we have to follow our heart. We might end up dying, but we die for love." To which the Christian might reply: "It is still possible to look for love in the wrong place. Let me show you the place where love can really be found." And that place would be where God himself died for love–at the cross of Christ.

Homosexuality and pure sex

Through what Christ has done on the cross, there is the possibility of change and healing for all humanity. Through him, even the notoriously immoral Corinthians could receive a new start, be washed clean, declared guiltless, and set apart as God's own people. The liberating message of biblical Christianity applies every bit as

---

7. Satinover, pp. 49-51.

8. Schmidt's catalogue of the destructive consequences of the gay lifestyle (in *Straight and Narrow*, chapter 6) is even more detailed and damning than Satinover's. Schmidt documents his conclusions by drawing upon nearly 200 scholarly, secular medical and social scientific publications representing the most recent research into problems associated with homosexuality. Moreover, none of these sources are Christian–in fact virtually all are either neutral or affirming toward homosexuality. Yet the combined picture they paint is as breathtaking as it is tragic.

much to those struggling with homosexuality as to those battling with any other form of sinful behaviour.

The difficulty we face as the new millennium dawns is swimming against the tide of pro-gay sentiment in which our society is awash–such has been the power and success of the gay lobby in influencing the public discourse. In one sense, the purpose of this appendix has been at least to begin to counteract some of the propaganda, and to present a more accurate appraisal.

In doing so, we have said very little about the real personal struggles many people have with homosexuality. One of the difficulties is that (as a result of gay activism) the idea has entered popular culture that to be gay is an inherent, inborn, inescapable personality trait. It is argued that once you start to experience homosexual feelings, or to have some homoerotic experience, it is useless to resist the inevitable. You are gay–that's all there is to it. You can yield to your true nature, or else struggle against it in frustration, hypocrisy and self-loathing for the rest of your life.

Like much gay propaganda, this is very misleading. It is certainly true that most people who pursue a homosexual lifestyle do not simply choose to do so casually, on a whim, or for no particular reason. There is a cluster of influences that pushes people towards homosexuality–including some genetic and biological traits that can make males feel 'different' (such as sensitivity, creativity, a heightened aesthetic sense), childhood experiences of alienation from other males (especially in relation to fathers), childhood experiences of sexual abuse, homoerotic experiences in puberty, and so on.

Having been pushed in this direction by a variety of factors, the actual step into an active homosexual lifestyle feels not like a choice but like an acceptance of the inevitable. Yet it is not inevitable–any more than a descent into alcoholism is inevitable. The two paths are quite similar. All sorts of biological, family and social factors may predispose someone towards alcoholism, but the descent into compulsive and addictive behaviour happens one deliberate step at a time, until the point is reached where it feels almost impossible to turn back. The key is not to start down the road, and to deal with the underlying problems that are pushing you in that direction; or if you are already down the road, to admit the problem, to take dramatic action, and to deal with the underlying issues.

All this is terribly brief and doubtless inadequate for those readers who might be struggling personally with homosexual feelings or desires. We would recommend books such as Schmidt's and Satinover's (see the footnotes) for a more detailed and helpful treatment of the issues. More helpful still would be to contact one of the many organizations that specialize in helping people through these struggles.[9]

The personal struggles for some are very real, and painful. The struggle for us as a society is just as real. Under the intense and ongoing pressure of gay political activism, we have accepted the 'normalization' of homosexuality. Vice, said Alexander Pope, is a frightful monster who only needs to be seen once to be hated...

> Yet seen too oft, familiar with her face,
> We first endure, then pity, then embrace.

---

9. Please contact the publisher for details of these organizations in your local area.

APPENDIX 2

Two ways to live

In the course of this book, and in particular in chapter 6, we confronted the issue of rebellion against God, and the need to turn back to him. We dealt with the subject only briefly, and some readers may wish to know more.

What follows is a more detailed explanation of the Bible's basic teaching about where humans stand before God, where Jesus fits into this, and how we can turn back to God.

There are six basic points to be made.

1. God—the loving ruler and creator

The first point of the Christian message is that God is in charge of the world. He is the ruler, the supreme president, the king. Unlike human rulers, however, God always does what is best for his subjects. He is the kind of king you'd like to be ruled by.

God rules the world because he made the world. Like a potter with his clay, God fashioned the world into just the shape he wished, with all its amazing details. He made it, and he owns it.

He also made us. God created people who were something like himself, and put them in charge of the world–to rule it, to care for it, to be responsible for it, and to enjoy all its beauty and goodness. He appointed humanity to supervise and look after the world, but always under his own authority, honouring him and obeying his directions.

As the Bible puts it:

> You are worthy, our Lord and God, to receive glory and honour and power, for you created all things, and by your will they were created and have their being (Revelation 4:11).

It all sounds rather ideal–God in heaven, people ruling the world according to his directions, and everything right with the world. But everything is very obviously not right–with us or the world.

2. Humanity in rebellion

The sad truth is that, from the very beginning, men and women everywhere have rejected God by doing things their own way. We all do this. We don't like someone telling us what to do or how to live–least of all God–and so we rebel against him in lots of different ways. We ignore him and just get on with our own lives; or we disobey his instructions for living in his world; or we shake our puny fists in his face and tell him to get lost.

How ever we do it, we are all rebels, because we don't live God's way. We prefer to follow our own desires, and to run things our own way, without God. This rebellious, self-sufficient attitude is what the Bible calls 'sin'.

The trouble is, in rejecting God we make a mess not only of our own lives, but of our society and the world. The whole world is full of people bent on doing what suits **them**, and not following God's ways. We all act like little gods, with our own crowns, competing with one another. The result is misery. The suffering and injustice that we see around us all go back to our basic rebellion against God.

> Jesus went on: "What comes out of a man is what makes him 'unclean'. For from within, out of men's hearts, come evil thoughts, sexual immorality, theft, murder, adultery, greed, malice, deceit, lewdness, envy, slander, arrogance and folly" (Mark 7:20-22).

> There is no-one righteous, not even one; there is no-one who understands, no-one who seeks God. All have turned away (Romans 3:10-12).

By rebelling against God, we've made a terrible mess of things. The question is: what will God do about it?

3. God gives rebels what they ask for

God cares enough about humanity to take our rebellion seriously. He calls us to account for our actions, because it matters to him that we treat him, and other people, so poorly. In other words, he won't let the rebellion go on forever.

The sentence God passes against us is entirely just, because he gives us exactly what we ask for. In rebelling against God, we are saying to him, "Go away. I don't want you telling me what to do. Leave me alone." And this is precisely what God does. His judgement on rebels is to withdraw from them, to cut them off from himself–permanently. But since God is the source of life and all good things, being cut off from him means death and hell. God's judgement against rebels is an everlasting, God-less death.

This is a terrible thing, to fall under the sentence of God's judgement. It is a prospect we all face, since we are all guilty of rebelling against God.

> He will punish those who do not know God and do not obey the gospel of our Lord Jesus. They will be punished with everlasting destruction and shut out from the presence of the Lord and from the majesty of his power (2 Thessalonians 1:8-9).

> Man is destined to die once, and after that to face judgment (Hebrews 9:27).

Is that it then? Are we all destined for death and everlasting ruin? If not for God's own miraculous intervention, we would be.

4. Jesus—the Man who dies for rebels

Because of his great love and generosity, God did not leave us to suffer the consequences of our foolish rebellion. He did something to save us. He sent his own divine son into our world to become a man–Jesus of Nazareth.

Unlike us, Jesus didn't rebel against God. He always lived under God's rule. He always did what God said, and so did not deserve death or punishment. Yet Jesus did die. Although he had the power of God to heal the sick, walk on water and even raise the dead, Jesus allowed himself to be executed on a cross. Why?

The Bible rings with the incredible news that **Jesus died as a substitute for rebels like us**. The debt that we owed God, Jesus paid by dying in our place. He took the full force of God's justice on himself, so that forgiveness and pardon might be available to us.

All this is quite undeserved by us. It is a generous gift, from start to finish.

> Christ died for sins once for all, the righteous for the unrighteous, to bring you to God (1 Peter 3:18).

> He himself bore our sins in his body on the tree, so that we might die to sins and live for righteousness; by his wounds you have been healed (1 Peter 2:24).

But that's not all.

5. Jesus—the risen ruler

God accepted Jesus' death as payment in full for our sins, and **raised him from the dead**. The risen Jesus is now what humanity was always meant to be: God's ruler of the world.

As God's ruler, Jesus has also been appointed God's judge of the world. The Bible promises that one day, he will return to call all of us to account for our actions.

In the meantime, Jesus offers us new life, both now and eternally. Now, our sins can be forgiven through Jesus' death, and we can make a fresh start with God, no longer as rebels but as friends. In this new life, God himself comes to live within us by his Spirit. We can experience the joy of a new relationship with God.

What's more, when we are pardoned through Jesus' death, we can be quite sure that when Jesus does return to judge, we will be acceptable to him. The risen Jesus will give us eternal life, not because we have earned it, but because he has died in our place.

> For he has set a day when he will judge the world with justice by the man he has appointed. He has given proof of this to all men by raising him from the dead (Acts 17:31).

> Praise be to the God and Father of our Lord Jesus Christ! In his great mercy he has given us new birth into a living hope through the resurrection of Jesus Christ from the dead (1 Peter 1:3).

Well, where does all that leave us? It leaves us with a choice of only two ways to live.

6. Two ways to live

The message of Christianity is not academic or theoretical. In the end it demands a response. It presents us with only two ways to live.

1. We can continue in our rebellion against God, and try to run our lives our own way without him. Sadly, this is the option that many people persist in.

The end result is that God gives us what we ask for and deserve. He condemns us for our rejection of his rightful rule over our lives. We not only have to put up with the messy consequences of rejecting God here and now, but we face the dreadful prospect of an eternity of separation from him, without life or love or relationship.

2. For those of us who have realised that our situation is hopeless, there is a lifeline. If we turn back to God and appeal for mercy, trusting in Jesus' death and resurrection, then everything changes.

For a start, God wipes our slate clean. He accepts Jesus' death as payment for our sins, and freely and completely forgives us. He pours his own Spirit into our hearts and grants us a new life that stretches past death and into forever. We are no longer rebels, but part of God's own family as his adopted sons and daughters. We now live with Jesus as our ruler.

> Whoever believes in the Son has eternal life, but whoever rejects the Son will not see life, for God's wrath remains on him (John 3:36).

> For God so loved the world that he gave his one and only Son, that whoever believes in him shall not perish but have eternal life (John 3:16).

Which of these two ways represents how you want to live?

Over to you

The two ways to live could not be more different, and they present you, the reader, with some choices.

If your answer to the question above is 'my own way', then you probably don't believe some or all of the message we have been outlining. Perhaps you do not believe that God is going to judge rebels, or that you really are a rebel. If that is the case, then please think carefully. It would be a good idea to investigate what we have been saying thoroughly, because if it is true, the consequences are life and death. Perhaps you could get hold of a modern translation of the Bible and read about it for yourself (Mark's Gospel is a good place to start). Or you could talk to a Christian friend, or your local minister.

However, if you know that you are a rebel against God, and would prefer to live his way, the next obvious question is: **What can you do about it?**

What to do

The first thing to do is to talk to God. You need to admit before him that you have rebelled against him, that you deserve punishment, and that you're asking for mercy on the basis of Jesus' death in your place. You'll also need to ask God to help you change from being a rebel to being someone who lives with Jesus as their ruler. You could pray something like this:

> *Dear God,*
>
> *I know that I am not worthy to be accepted by you. I don't deserve your gift of eternal life. I am guilty of rebelling against you and ignoring you. I need forgiveness.*
>
> *Thank you for sending your son to die for me that I may be forgiven. Thank you that he rose from the dead to give me new life.*
>
> *Please forgive me and change me, that I may live with Jesus as my ruler. Amen.*

The first step, then, is to pray.

The second step is also fairly obvious. Having prayed the sort of prayer above, you will want to start putting it into practice–that is, actually submitting to Jesus. There will no doubt be all kinds of areas in your life in need of change. You'll need to get rid of old rebellious habits (like greed, anger, selfishness, and so on) and start some new ones that please God (like generosity, kindness, love and patience). This second step will go on for the rest of your life, but God will be with you all the way. He'll keep speaking to you (through your reading of the Bible); he'll keep listening to you and helping you (as you pray to him); he'll empower you to change and to live his way (by his Spirit that lives within you); and he'll provide brothers and sisters to encourage you along the way (as you meet with other Christians).

The second step, then, is to submit to Jesus and start living with him as your ruler.

The third thing you have to do is also ongoing. You need to keep putting your trust in the right place. It's only because of Jesus (and his death and resurrection) that you can be forgiven and put right with God. You'll need to keep coming back to this again and again, because as you start to live God's new way, you will still fail and do the wrong thing. We all do. We all need to keep looking back to the death of Jesus on the cross as the only grounds for our pardon. We must never stop relying on him–and him alone–as the means by which we are forgiven and granted eternal life.

If you know full well that you have not yet taken these steps, and that you are still an unforgiven rebel, then you need to do something about it. You are at a fork in the road. It's the choice that we all face. There are only two ways to live.

For further information, please write to:
Matthias Media
PO Box 225
Kingsford NSW 2032
or email us at <matmedia@ozemail.com.au>.

About Matthias Media

Ever since ‘St Matthias Press and Tapes’ first opened its doors in 1988, under the auspices of St Matthias Anglican Church, Centennial Park, in Sydney, our aim has been to provide the Christian community with products of a uniformly high standard—both in their biblical faithfulness and in the quality of the writing and production.

Now known as Matthias Media, we have grown to become a nationwide provider of user-friendly resources for ministry, with Christians of all sorts using our Bible studies, books, Briefings, audio cassettes, videos, training courses—you name it.

For more information about the range of Matthias Media resources, call us on Freecall 1800 814 360 (or in Sydney 9663-1478), or fax us on (02) 9662-4289, and we will send you a free catalogue. Or you can e-mail us at <matmedia@ozemail.com.au>. Or visit our Web site at:

http://www.gospelnet.com.au/matmedia/

Buy direct from us and save

If you order your Matthias Media resources direct from us, you not only save time and money, you invest in more great resources for the future:

- you save time—we usually despatch our orders within 24 hours of receiving them
- you save money—our normal prices are better than other retailers' prices (plus if you order in bulk, you'll save even more)
- you help keep us afloat—because we get more from each sale, buying from us direct helps us to stay alive in the difficult world of publishing.

A Fresh Start by John Chapman

Something is terribly wrong—with our world, with our relationships, with us. We all sense this at different times. But is there anything that can be done about it?

With all the honesty and humour for which he is famous, John Chapman tells us in *A Fresh Start* that God has done something about it. We read about:

- just what God has done for us through his Son, Jesus;
- how we can know it is true;
- what the alternatives are;
- and what we should do about it.

If you have been searching for a book that simply and clearly explains what it means to be a Christian, either for your own or another's benefit, your search is over.

Guidance and the Voice of God

by Phillip D. Jensen & Tony Payne

- How do I know what God wants me to do?
- How can I make decisions which are in line with his will?
- If God speaks to me, will I recognize his voice?

These are important questions, and many Christians grapple with them. Guidance and the Voice of God charts a way through these often confusing issues, and shows how for those who have ears to hear, God is still speaking loud and clear through his Son.

Look for these title in your local Christian bookstore, or order direct from Matthias Media by calling us tollfree on 1800 814 360 (9663-1478 in Sydney).